Agile Change
Management

Agile Change Management

A practical framework for successful change planning and implementation

MELANIE FRANKLIN

KoganPage

LONDON PHILADELPHIA NEW DELHI

First published in Great Britain and the United States in 2014 by Kogan Page Limited

2nd Floor, 45 Gee Street
London EC1V 3RS
United Kingdom
www.koganpage.com

1518 Walnut Street, Suite 1100
Philadelphia PA 19102
USA

4737/23 Ansari Road
Daryaganj
New Delhi 110002
India

© Melanie Franklin, 2014

ISBN   978 0 7494 7098 2
E-ISBN   978 0 7494 7099 9

British Library Cataloguing-in-Publication Data

A CIP record for this book is available from the British Library.

Library of Congress Cataloging-in-Publication Data

Franklin, Melanie
   Agile change management : a practical framework for successful change planning and implementation / Melanie Franklin.
      pages cm
      ISBN 978-0-7494-7098-2 (pbk.) – ISBN 978-0-7494-7099-9 (ebk)   1. Organizational change–Management.   I. Title.
   HD58.8.F7125 2014
   658.4'06–dc23
                                                                                2013049646

Typeset by Graphicraft Limited, Hong Kong
Print production managed by Jellyfish

Contents

Online resources to accompany this book are available from
www.koganpage.com/agilechangemanagement

Introduction

You cannot succeed if you do not know how to change what you do today to keep pace with changes taking place everywhere. Change management is not a specialist role – it is core to *every* role in an organization. The ability to design and implement change easily and realize its benefits quickly is at the core of survival and competitive advantage.

This book is for everyone involved in making change happen in organizations. Change is anything new or different, which involves creating new ways of working as we try to unlearn how we used to work, whilst continuing to provide business as usual to everyone who relies on us – a mixture of external clients, our suppliers and partner organizations and our colleagues. My aim was to create a practical guide to all aspects of change, not just the method to be used, but also to share ideas about how to support ourselves and others through the psychological impact of change, which is considerable but often overlooked.

Our relationships with others and our ability to empathize, influence and motivate them is at the heart of making change happen. If we cannot persuade others to do things differently then change will simply not happen. It doesn't matter if it is strategically important, or has been created according to best practice methods and techniques, people will always resist change that hasn't engaged them emotionally.

There is a huge body of work from psychologists, consultants and HR practitioners that explains the many theories of how the human brain works, what motivates us, what causes us to resist change, and suggests techniques for building rapport and emotional engagement. I have tried to synthesize much of this material into an easy-to-read guide on creating supportive working environments and building effective relationships.

Underpinning everything that I have written is my knowledge that without participation and involvement from everyone who is affected by the change we are implementing, the change will never become embedded into how people work, and will not replace the manner in which work is currently done.

In a career spanning more than 20 years, I have sponsored, managed and led countless change initiatives and the one determinant between success and failure, which is common to all of these changes, is the level of participation across all job roles and all levels of seniority both inside and outside the affected organization.

As well as generating participation, we need to ensure that whatever type of change we are trying to make, it adds value and is of benefit to our organization as a whole and to all those impacted by it. In recent years a lot of material on managing and realizing benefits has been published. These books and articles set out useful processes for identifying and measuring benefits and give step-by-step guidance for the activities involved. However, they all make the same assumption, which is that everyone knows what a business benefit is. In my experience, this is not the case, and many people involved in managing projects and defining change initiatives start by asking their customer what they want, and then create a plan to deliver it. They do not ask them why they want it, and they struggle to challenge those paying for the work to explain how what they are asking for is better than what is currently in place.

Without this debate on the business need and the business value to be delivered by change initiatives, we cannot get under the skin of what's involved, and we cannot provide enough depth to the question 'what's in it for me?' by those whose participation we need.

I have learnt from experience that whilst senior management commitment is an important factor in getting change initiatives off the ground, it is not enough to guarantee success. Translating ideas into new ways of working is best led by those closest to the changes. I haven't made specific reference to job titles in this book, but I have assumed you have specialist knowledge about how to carry out a specific task or role that is expected to be impacted by the change, so you are responsible for making the necessary changes.

I have picked up the story from the point when the need for the change has been defined by the senior management of your organization. The scope and objectives of the change have been explained at a high level, but the detailed planning of its implementation as it affects your department is your responsibility. This is because my intention is to explain how to make change happen, rather than to get caught up with explaining the strategic models and processes that lead an organization to change direction.

In your role you do not have authority over people and cannot 'force' them to participate in the change. Therefore, your ability to build productive relationships with your colleagues and create an environment that welcomes and supports change is going to be very important to the success of the change.

The change you are leading is likely to have an impact on your work, that of your immediate colleagues and possibly will also impact the department that you work in. I have assumed that you do not have authority or responsibility for implementing the change across the whole of your organization but if the change is organization-wide then you are a part of this effort.

My aim was to create a pragmatic guide to making change a reality, so I have concentrated on explaining how to create new ways of working, whilst acknowledging – rather than planning – how to create cultural change. These new ways of working will lead people to think and behave differently, and may include the adoption of new values and beliefs about their work. This 'cultural' change is a product of new ways of working and will manifest itself only when the change has been implemented and people have formed their own opinion of how the change affects them and how it makes them feel about their job and the organization they work for.

As well as your role in implementing change, you are expected to continue with your 'business as usual' role. You will need to split your time so that existing performance measures are met, whilst at the same time introducing changes to business as usual to create a new way of working for yourself and your colleagues. Alternatively, you are a project manager responsible for creating the deliverables that will form the new ways of working, and helping those who will use these deliverables to incorporate them into their day-to-day procedures and activities.

I haven't assumed that you have any prior knowledge or formal training in change management and although everything that I have written is derived from well-researched theories and commonly accepted best practice, I have put everything into my own words so this is not an academic book full of references. If you are interested in following up on more information, I have created a resources section (see page 269) listing the publications that I think give the best explanation of change.

To help you find what you need as quickly as possible, I have structured the book around four key themes. The themes are interlinked but you can pick up the story at any point:

- Theme 1 – Roadmap: an explanation of all the processes, activities and information needed to plan and manage any type of change initiative.

- Theme 2 – Business need: understanding what business value really means and how to acquire the information to ensure your change is making a beneficial contribution.

- Theme 3 – Building relationships: how to build trust and develop supportive relationships between all those impacted by change.

- Theme 4 – Creating the environment for change: how to establish a supportive environment that motivates people to participate in change.

The book is split into three parts:

1 Concept: the agile approach to managing change is explained and the principles of effective change are introduced.

2 Roadmap: the implementation of the change is described from the initial idea to its successful adoption. The roadmap organizes the change into a coherent timetable of activities and outcomes across three steps:

- getting started – understand why the change is needed, who is impacted by it and how they might contribute to its successful implementation;

Figure 0.1   Structure of the book

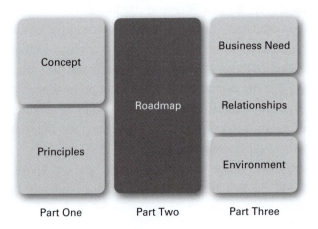

- making progress – identifying each of the activities needed to make the change a reality and how to involve people so that they take ownership for changing how they work;

- realizing benefits – how to complete the change and measure its effectiveness.

3 Skills: this explains the techniques and abilities needed to understand the impact of the change, create an environment that supports change and build partnerships with all those affected by it. These skills will be illustrated with practical tips and advice, with an explanation of why the skill is important and how it contributes to successful change.

Concept

01

Explaining agile working

The approach to managing change outlined in this book is based on the concept of agility. Agility means the ability to move quickly and easily. The concept of agile working has been adopted by many organizations which have realized that their hierarchical structures and lengthy decision-making processes are no longer fit for purpose in a world of complex and continuous change.

All change is complex because the environment in which we operate has become complex. There is so much interconnectivity between the systems, data and processes we use to carry out our role and the systems, as well as the data and processes of all those that we engage with including subsidiaries and our partners, suppliers, customers and regulators, that it is no longer possible to define what all of these connections are, so it is not possible to predict with any certainty what the impact of a change to one process or system will be on other processes or systems.

There are fewer easy answers to achieving our strategic goals. Greater economic uncertainty, the fast pace of technological change and the expectation of customers that organizations will tailor a solution to meet their individual needs has increased the volume of changes that we make to how we work. Whilst the pace of change today feels fast, it is unlikely to ever be this slow again.

The pace of change impacts the expected lifespan of any change that we make. The expected lifespan of each change becomes shorter as continuous innovation leads to continuous obsolescence. This means that we are under increasing pressure to ensure that the changes we make can pay back their costs and demonstrate a return on investment within the same financial year that they are implemented.

Figure 1.1 Increase in the pace of change

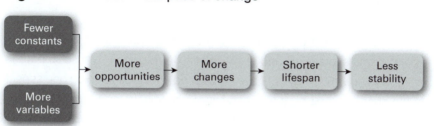

This volume means that change is continuous; it is no longer a special situation that is planned and resourced separately from our business as usual responsibilities. Change is no longer only conceived and implemented 'top down'. We are all responsible for doing our job and at the same time coming up with ways in which we can improve how we work.

Evolving solution

An agile approach is ideally suited to implementing change because of its emphasis on allowing the solution to evolve as the factors driving the need for change also evolve. Key to agile working is the acceptance that the change cannot be planned in detail at the start, but will need to emerge as more becomes known about the situation you are trying to improve (the business need) and the changes taking place in all aspects of your organization and the wider business environment that affect the situation.

Business need

The business need is the purpose of the change. It explains why the change is necessary and is a mixture of the expected improvements (benefits), the level of quality that the change must meet (acceptance criteria) and the features and functions that the change is expected to have (requirements).

Iterative process

It is better to try and change one thing and see what impact it has than to spend months planning and implementing a 'big idea' whose impact is unknown and which may not have the desired effect. Developing one aspect of the change, applying it to real business conditions and allowing people to assimilate how the change affects them brings greater results:

- the timeframe for implementing the change is reduced by avoiding all of the detailed planning upfront, and by encouraging those involved in the change to implement it in an incremental way, allowing changes to be adopted by the users as soon as they have been created, rather than waiting until the end of the change initiative and bundling them all together as a complete solution;

- there is an increase in the return on investment from the change because benefits can be realized as soon as the first elements of the change are incorporated into the business environment, so the change initiative starts to pay back its costs even before it has been completed.

Return on investment

This term refers to the measurement of the expected financial benefits from making the change, after the costs of planning, implementing and embedding the costs have been subtracted.

The volume of change taking place in our organizations increases the chances that requirements identified today will be out of date by the time a complex change initiative has implemented them. As soon as one requirement has been identified, it has been superseded by another idea. It is better to create an environment where there is regular and frequent discussion of what is needed, which is acted upon immediately. This also benefits those identifying the need for change because it releases them from the pressure of trying to predict every aspect of the future.

Iterative development

Iterative development concerns the creation of new ways of working as a series of versions, created sequentially, where each version builds on the content of the one before it. Later versions will include additional features and functions that were not created when the earlier versions were released to the users.

Planning only the outline of the change at the start and allowing the details to be defined as more becomes known about the situation ensures that the changes are fresh and up to date, which improves the overall quality of the change.

Collaboration

Agile working emphasizes the need to work collaboratively with all those involved in the change, including those with technical skills who create the solution and those in business roles who will use this solution as their new way of working.

Collaboration

Collaboration is a general term derived directly from the Latin words for 'working together'. It means organized sharing of information and activities.

Collaboration increases the workability of the solution because there is a shared understanding between those creating the elements of change (project teams, system suppliers, HR functions creating the new structure or redefining the performance measurement criteria etc) and those responsible for redefining their ways of working. This reduces the 'them and us' environment that is prevalent in many projects where the project team create a solution and throw it over the wall to the users at the end of the project, hoping that it will be implemented by them and benefits will be realized.

The pace of change, flexibility in the changes we make, frequent iterations and greater collaboration make an agile approach a powerful tool for the effective delivery of change. These themes will all be covered later in the book, as we explore how to apply the concept of agile working to the change initiatives we are responsible for.

Principles

02

In this chapter we will cover some simple rules for managing change. It is vital to understand how successful change happens in practice. To this end I asked some talented and successful change managers to tell me the things they always try to remember to do, and the things that if they don't remember to do they regret.

Five guiding principles

The five guiding principles are:

1 recognize that there is a deadline for making the change and respect it;

2 allow the details of the change to evolve;

3 ensure the change meets a business need;

4 work collaboratively across a wide spectrum of interested parties;

5 balance time and resources across all phases of the change.

These principles support an agile approach to change because their emphasis is on creating changes that evolve to meet the business need. The emphasis is on flexibility. The change programme is not defined in detail from the start, but relies on the collaborative efforts of all those impacted to agree what needs to change and implement these ideas piecemeal, always ready to halt the change initiative as soon as the solution is 'good enough'. This turns traditional approaches upside down, because instead of having a significant planning effort upfront, the emphasis is on developing the ideas and seeing what impact they have. Application of these principles is challenging because an agile approach does not present those funding or governing the change with a detailed understanding of what they are getting; they have to have faith that those involved will deliver improvements on an 'as needed' basis, and will not run late or overspend because they are adhering to the principles of on-time delivery and meeting a business need.

These principles align to the paradigm shift that is currently taking place, where change initiatives are becoming the new 'norm', embedded in the responsibilities of every member of staff rather than one-off initiatives run by specialists.

These principles underpin all of the guidance in this book. For example:

- Chapter 3: The roadmap is shaped by the need to deliver the change to the agreed timeframe and the need to allow the details of the change to emerge as the initiative progresses. These principles govern the importance of delivering at least a minimum amount of change during every timebox, and to ensure that change is implemented iteratively so that feedback from those impacted can be used to shape the next deployment of new ways of working. Delivering to an agreed timescale and evolving the solution drives the importance of the prioritization technique that shapes the content of each timebox.

- Chapter 3 also explains how to ensure that your change initiative does not become 'plan heavy' and that you balance the effort and involvement of all those concerned across the full lifecycle of the change, whilst at the same time maintaining an acceptable level of performance in business as usual.

- Chapter 4: Business need gives a detailed explanation of how the principle of creating change that meets the needs of those impacted is applied. Developing a detailed understanding of what is needed to satisfy the demands of your organization for efficient, high-quality work and the demands of your customers for innovative products and services is key to adhering to this principle. However, understanding business need is not a stand-alone principle. It must be supported by the principles of delivering to an agreed timeframe and evolving the solution as more becomes known about the business need.

- Effective change cannot be achieved in an atmosphere of 'them and us' where those creating the changes then impose their ideas on those using the changes. Chapters 6 and 7 explain how to create a shared understanding and an environment that supports collaborative working.

If you are ever in any doubt about the progress of your change initiative, review these principles as they will reconfirm your approach and help you to stay focused on your successful implementation.

1 Recognize that there is a deadline for making the change and respect it

What does the principle mean?

- Delivering on time is a critical success factor for any change initiative. Certainty of when change will take place allows those affected by it to prepare themselves and their environment for working in a new way.

- Failure to deliver on time can eradicate the benefits that the change is expected to realize. This is because delays to the implementation of change delay the start of any improvements, which are the benefits that will pay for the changes.

What are the activities?

- The timeframe must be agreed between those who need the change and those who will implement the change, taking into account the needs of their marketplace, their customers and their own internal deadlines.

- The time allowed for the change initiative must be divided across each of the iterations of the change, and then flow down to control each of the processes of the change. Finally it must also flow down into each of the timeboxes, ie periods of concentrated effort when the changes are created. The roadmap explained on page 18 shows how this is achieved.

How does the principle contribute to effective change?

- It enables the business to plan the most effective use of resources between implementing the change and maintaining acceptable levels of service for customers through business as usual activities.

2 Allow the details of the change to evolve

What does the principle mean?

- It is not possible to predict with sufficient certainty what all of the elements of the change are. Once change begins to take place, further enhancements and amendments will be identified.

- This principle supports efficient use of resources. It encourages those responsible for implementing change to plan the detail when it is required – there's no need to resource a detailed planning effort at the start of the change.

- This removes false certainty from the change initiative, as a detailed plan creates the impression that all factors are fixed and agreed and does not allow for evolution of the original ideas.

What are the activities?

- Balance this level of uncertainty by ensuring that whatever changes are delivered, are delivered on time.

- Ensure that all those involved in the change recognize that they will need to be involved throughout the full lifecycle of the change as it will be implemented incrementally, as each requirement is fulfilled. This enables those affected by the change to provide feedback on what is working well and what other changes are required.

How does the principle contribute to effective change?

- The principles and actions allow the change to evolve and deliver each part of the change incrementally as soon as it is ready for use. It negates the need to make people wait until the end of the change project ensuring that they can adjust to each of the changes, adapt it to their needs and get ready for the next change because the impact of change can be big even if the content of the change is small.

3 Ensure that the change meets a business need

What does the principle mean?

- Change is costly and its disruption to business as usual can be very risky for the organization. There must be strong reasons for changing the status quo and it must have the commitment of senior managers who will authorize and fund the changes.

What are the activities?

- To ensure that the perceived need for change is real, it's important to test the ideas against internal requirements and external market and/or customer requirements. Assess the impact of the change so that where possible it has a positive impact on those working in the organization and external parties that rely on the organization for the provision of products and services.

How does the principle contribute to effective change?

- An imbalance between internal and external drivers for change can mean that the change is skewed towards too narrow a group of recipients and will generate too little business value to justify the cost.

4 Work collaboratively across a wide spectrum of interested parties

What does the principle mean?

- The most successful change initiatives have the full participation of everyone who is impacted. The level of contribution varies from person to person, but making the change a reality is a team effort, and you cannot force the change onto others, however persuasive you are.

What are the activities?

- Make sure that the change activities are on every agenda of every meeting, so that talking about the change becomes the 'norm'.
- Make sure the change activities are designed to appeal to every level of staff and manager. Senior management commitment is often cited as a critical success factor for change initiatives, but the commitment of new joiners, the newly promoted and the staff that have been in situ for years are just as important.
- Treat participation levels as an important performance measure for the change initiative. This is not the time to act the martyr or have the

attitude that 'it is quicker to do it myself' or 'I haven't got time to explain what needs to be done, I just need to get it done'.

How does the principle contribute to effective change?

- It creates shared understanding of what is needed between those creating the new ways of working and those impacted by them.
- It enables those creating the changes and those implementing them to support each other throughout the change lifecycle, so there is no hiatus at the end of the development work whilst those impacted are brought up to speed with information about the initiative.

5 Balance time and resources across all phases of the change

What does the principle mean?

- Emphasis is often given to the conception and planning of change with the level of commitment and energy tailing off as the initiative progresses. This is counterintuitive, because it is once the change initiative has commenced and changes are being implemented that the greatest resources are required. This is the point at which resistance to change will be expressed and where those implementing the change will need to persevere in the face of this opposition, creatively overcome difficulties and address the gaps between expectation and reality.
- It is during the implementation of change that the majority of people become impacted by the change and significant resources will be required to guide and manage their participation and ensure that they have all of the information that they need.

What are the activities?

- Accept that being involved in any change means dividing your time, your effort and your attention between the current situation (your day job) and all the things that create the future (the change activities). If you don't get the balance right then either the change will not be successful, or business as usual will fall below acceptable performance levels.

- Clarify when you plan to focus on change and when you plan to focus on business as usual so others can plan their engagement with you.

- When planning the change, remember to pace yourself and the contribution of your colleagues so that energy is retained for later in the change lifecycle. Your change cannot be successful if all of the energy and commitment is given to the initial scoping, and early deployments, with nothing left for the later embedding of the change.

How does the principle contribute to effective change?

- Ensuring that effort is balanced across all phases of change means that there will be sufficient attention paid to the need for the change, its scope and objectives, and identification of those needed to participate. It also provides the opportunity to create an environment that encourages the implementation of the change.

- Successful change requires resilience and perseverance, and the requirements for these qualities grows as the change progresses. Ensuring that sufficient resources are available right up until the last activity has been completed is essential for ensuring that the change will be fully adopted to create the new business as usual environment.

These principles help you to interpret what working in an agile way means for your change. This agility ensures that the changes you create continue to evolve to meet the needs of your organization and have the greatest possible chance of realizing the benefits that are expected.

Agile change enables you to make a positive contribution to your organization in an era dominated by complex, continuous change, where the capability for successful implementation of change is a significant competitive advantage.

Roadmap

Introduction

This chapter outlines the content of a roadmap, which defines the steps needed to manage the change from initial idea to successful implementation. In this book I have called this step-by-step guide a roadmap, but it could equally be called an approach, a framework or a methodology. It doesn't matter what the terminology is, we are only interested in the improvements that it brings to the implementation of change.

In highly performing organizations, the governance of change is a core element of the operating processes. Each function or department manages change in the same way, having recognized that managing change is no longer a one-off exercise but is a routine part of everyday business life. These organizations have confidence in their ability to deliver change and realize benefits and have developed their own frameworks or roadmaps that define their approach.

However, for the majority of organizations, change is still managed ad hoc, with managers given little central support and expected to work out for themselves how to cope with change. Whilst the need to build a capability for managing change is recognized, it is at an early stage and the comprehensive resources that exist for other management disciplines do not yet exist for managing change.

This chapter seeks to address this shortfall by providing you with an approach that you can adopt for yourself to enable you to get started and to see the change through to a successful conclusion. It is consistent with the agile approach outlined in Chapter 2. This chapter:

- assumes the nature of the change will be driven by business need and not by what is technically possible or how the organization usually does things;

- encourages incremental delivery of the change, with each new way of working adding to what has already been changed;
- relies on collaboration between all those involved and encourages them to be empowered to direct their own work without relying on a high degree of central control;
- sets time as the constraint recognizing that a workable solution delivered early is better than a 'perfect' solution delivered at some unspecified date in the future.

There is a lot of information to convey in this chapter so I have divided it into the following sections:

- Part 1: Developing a roadmap
  - considerations for use;
  - using the roadmap.
- Part 2: Applying the roadmap to your change
  - Iteration 1;
  - all other iterations.

Part 1: Developing a roadmap

Considerations for use

In this section I will explain what information a roadmap contains, how it fits with other aspects of your organization and what the benefits of having a roadmap are.

What information does a roadmap provide?

A roadmap sets out what needs to be done, who will be involved and what activities will be carried out. It should give you a step-by-step guide to managing all types of organizational change, and be flexible enough that it can be shaped to reflect the needs of your change, whilst still undertaking the core activities that need to apply to all changes.

Whilst the roadmap appears as a linear set of instructions, it has been designed to incorporate elements of agile working:

- don't try to understand everything at once – recognize that the picture will evolve as more information becomes available;

- share your understanding with others at an early stage so that you get access to their feedback;

- be proactive – ask other people what their impression of the change is and include their views in subsequent iterations of the work;

- constantly prioritize the change activities so that those activities most closely related to the realization of benefits are undertaken first.

Who are the users of the roadmap?

The contents of the roadmap need to meet the needs of different audiences (Figure 3.1):

1 You – as someone who is going to lead change in your area it should contain sensible, logical steps for you to follow that are easy to understand and remember. The roadmap will be of no use to you if it is so complex that you have to look up each next step.

2 Participants – those who need to become involved in the change will find it easier to understand what is required of them and when they are expected to participate as they can use the roadmap to identify what has already been done and what the next steps are. Information about how the change will be managed using the roadmap can be easily communicated to all those impacted by the change.

3 Change sponsor – the person that has overall accountability and responsibility for implementing the change and ensuring that the expected benefits are realized will benefit from an agreed approach so that they know when their intervention is likely to be required and when they should delegate tasks to those leading and participating in the change. Information about how the change will be managed using the roadmap can be easily communicated to the wider group of senior stakeholders with an interest in the success of the change.

4 Auditor – anyone who has a quality management or audit responsibility and needs to be able to understand what is supposed to take place during a change initiative and the basis on which decisions are taken and by whom.

Figure 3.1 Roadmap users

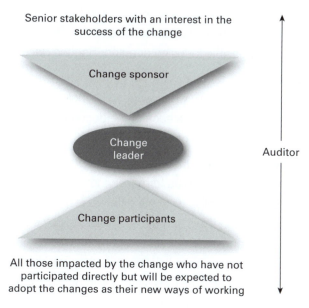

What are the core elements of a roadmap?

A simple roadmap shows the core elements of process and techniques. When you are tailoring this to meet your own needs it would be a good idea to give more information to your users to make it as easy as possible for them to get involved in managing their changes. Suggestions for all the elements of a roadmap are shown here:

1 **Processes** – a collection of activities that, taken together, create an important achievement in the life of the change initiative. These activities will be a mixture of 'doing' activities that implement the change and 'decisions' that authorize a particular course of action.

2 **Best practice techniques** – an explanation of how to carry out certain tasks within the change. These techniques include activities for generating participation in the change, eg facilitation of workshops, and specialist aspects of the change such as holding product demonstrations.

3 **Document templates** – to ensure all changes are managed on a like-for-like basis there needs to be an agreed set of documentation and an understanding of who is responsible for defining its content and who is responsible for using or authorizing the document.

4 **Guidance notes** – templates are no good unless everyone using them understands exactly what needs to be included. Guidance should be created to explain each of the document headings and to give examples of the type of content expected.

5 **Role definitions** – whilst the majority of people participating in the change are unlikely to take up formal change team roles, the roadmap should establish what the different responsibilities are, and how information flows and decision-making powers should be arranged amongst them. Even if a person takes on these responsibilities in addition to their day job, they still need to be able to understand how their work fits in with other people who are also working on the change.

6 **Role questionnaires** – a list of points to consider to help identify the right person to take on a role within the change initiative. For a definition of the roles see Appendix 1.

7 **Checklists** – these are an effective tool for ensuring that tasks have been completed, information has been gathered and the right people have been selected for their roles. Checklists might include:

   – completion checklists – before exiting each of the processes in your step-by-step guide, review to make sure that you have carried out each of the activities;

   – readiness checklists – before authorizing the deployment of new ways of working, ensure all preparation activities have been completed.

8 **Acceptance criteria** – before creating any of the outputs associated with your change, define what 'good' looks like by establishing a set of acceptance criteria that the output must meet if it is to be signed off as complete. These acceptance criteria can be created for the outputs associated with managing and governing the change, eg the risk register or the change plan and should also be created for each of the outputs specific to your change.

Points to consider

Does your organization have a culture of creating tool kits containing this type of information to help managers?

What elements of the roadmap are the most important for your change?

What are the acceptance criteria for an effective roadmap?

To check that your roadmap is delivering what it needs to, consider how well it meets the following criteria:

- The roadmap is a simple, intuitive process that everyone involved can follow. The roadmap should not be for the exclusive use of 'change management professionals' as very few of those impacted by the change will be formally trained in change management techniques. They are involved in the change because it is their ways of working that have to change, so they need a roadmap that suggests what they should be doing and what the next few steps are going to be in an easy to understand format.

- The roadmap has defined all of the activities required to implement change so that any interdependencies between the activities have been taken into account and to make sure that nothing has been forgotten. The roadmap must contain a comprehensive list of activities relevant to any type of change to enable those leading the change to make informed decisions about what is needed, minimizing the risk that they will miss out vital steps. There is considerable impact of failing to consider all of the work involved, reducing the accuracy of estimates of when the change will take place and reducing the quality of new ways of working.

- The roadmap organizes all of the work in a logical way so that the outputs from one step will contribute to the outputs from the next step. Implementing change is an incremental process and we need to build on each success that we have whilst minimizing the disruption to business as usual.

- The roadmap enables you to look ahead and recognize what is coming up next so that you can ask questions and proactively prepare for the next steps. To control the evolving solution we need to prioritize the work, and knowing what is involved in each step of the change enables you to make an informed decision about whether an activity must be carried out now or would be better left until later in the change where the work would be a better fit for the later activities and outputs.

- The points at which decisions need to be taken or progress can be measured are clearly defined so that the process is not allowed to run on unchecked. These review points allow progress to be tracked against the agreed timescales for the change, and if a decision point has not yet been reached it is easier to step in and take remedial action rather than letting the change initiative continue.

Where does the roadmap fit with other elements of your organization?

The day-to-day work of your organization is underpinned by an agreed way of doing things that includes a moral code or set of values and a quality system consisting of standards, processes and regulations that must be adhered to. Even if you have to create your own change roadmap because there is nothing 'official' in your organization, it is still important to make sure that it aligns to this infrastructure.

Core values

Aligning your roadmap of change activities to your organization's values and ethics gives your approach to change credibility and will reassure those responsible for the ethical operation of your organization that your work does not run counter to their ideas.

Whilst these value statements are unique to your organization, effective values often include some core statements that I have used to show you how to describe your roadmap in terms that link it to your organizational values:

Value 1 – We act with integrity, fairness and honesty

Use of the roadmap supports fairness in that each change initiative is managed in the same way, providing a consistency and a clear explanation of what is going to happen and when and in what order. This openness supports the core value of honesty, which is also described by many organizations as a desire for open communication.

Value 2 – We value our people and empower them to do a great job

Use of the roadmap empowers all those who believe they should be involved in the change initiative as they can understand what work is involved and decide for themselves how they can best contribute to this effort.

Value 3 – We understand and actively manage our risks

Risk management requires a willingness to look ahead and identify potential problems and act on them before they are able to affect the work. The roadmap supports this proactive stance by setting out what should be happening and allowing people to see where problems might arise and dealing with them early in the life of the change initiative.

Value 4 – We consistently exceed customer expectations by providing innovative solutions

The existence of a change roadmap sends the message that the organization is committed to change and has invested in its capability to routinely deliver new products, services and ways of working.

Quality system

Incorporating existing standards and regulations into your roadmap ensures that the way in which you implement your change aligns to agreed best practice in your organization.

By following a roadmap you establish from the beginning how the change will be managed, which means your actions can be reviewed against the roadmap and any discrepancies addressed, ensuring the quality of your management activities.

It also minimizes the risk that what is created by the change leads to a destabilization of business as usual, with some work conforming to standards and the newer ways of working operating outside of these constraints.

> ## Points to consider
>
> - What are the core values of your organization?
>
> - How are these communicated to managers and staff?
>
> - How can these be used to guide the scope of the change you are involved in?

What are the benefits of a roadmap?

Deciding on a standard approach for managing change requires time and effort to design and agree all of the steps. This effort is worthwhile as each change initiative benefits from using the roadmap. As with any change to how things are done, it is important to appreciate the benefits of having a roadmap so that you can explain them to others and get their support for your approach.

Whilst you will need to tailor these benefits statements to reflect your own circumstances, the benefits of a roadmap include the following.

Building the confidence of all those involved in change

Confidence comes from knowing what we are supposed to be doing, and how we are supposed to do it and knowing that we are following the best course of action.

The roadmap sets out everything you need to be doing from when the change is first proposed to its successful conclusion as the new way of working for your organization. It has been written to cover every type of change, from an imposed change such as meeting the requirements of new legislation to internally driven changes for creating new products and services. This provides you with a complete menu of ideas from which you can select what is best for your situation, enabling you to appear knowledgeable and in control of events even if you are doing something for the first time. This will inspire your own confidence and the confidence of those working with you.

Use of a roadmap can also increase the confidence of those responsible for sponsoring and taking decisions about the change. Throughout the life of the change decisions will need to be taken about:

- whether the change is needed;
- who should be involved in leading the effort;
- whether what has been created is fit for purpose and should be implemented.

It is easier to take these decisions if the information that supports them has been created as the result of a structured and pre-agreed process. Faster decisions can be made as the activities are the same for each change initiative, which builds confidence in them and provides a body of like for like information.

The roadmap also provides you with a mechanism for checking your progress. At any time you can step back from creating the new ways of working to check whether you have forgotten any steps and to identify what you should be doing next. This allows you to become fully immersed in what you are doing and allows you to be innovative and creative about your solutions instead of spending your creative energy devising what to do next.

Knowing what you should be doing enables you to plan your workload and balance your change activities against the requirements of your business as usual role. This reinforces your belief that you can achieve what is expected of you, and it helps you to manage the expectations of those around you in terms of the demands they can make on your time and the contribution that you are able to make whilst understanding what help you will need from them and when you are likely to need their assistance.

The roadmap in this book has been tried and tested in many different change initiatives by many change management professionals. I have been working in this field for over 20 years with lots of talented people and many of the actions included in the roadmap have been learnt the hard way, from doing the opposite of what the book recommends and then trying to put things right! So you can be reassured that you are using a best practice approach that is the product of a lot of experience and consolidation of lessons learned.

Improved return on investment

Using the roadmap encourages everyone involved in the change to understand its business value and to speak up if they think that the work they are doing is not likely to deliver the benefits required. This minimizes wasted effort, as only those activities most likely to add value are included in the change initiative.

This concentration of effort takes place not just at the start of the change, when everyone is concentrating on what to do, but during every step. By using the MoSCoW technique (Figure 3.2) decisions are frequently taken on whether something is a must have element of the change or is something that could be left out if resources are running low.

Figure 3.2 Summary of the MoSCoW technique

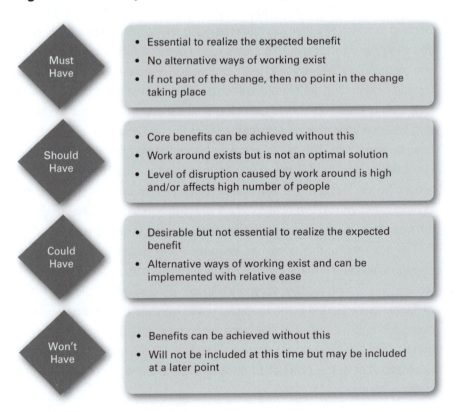

- Essential to realize the expected benefit
- No alternative ways of working exist
- If not part of the change, then no point in the change taking place

Must Have

- Core benefits can be achieved without this
- Work around exists but is not an optimal solution
- Level of disruption caused by work around is high and/or affects high number of people

Should Have

- Desirable but not essential to realize the expected benefit
- Alternative ways of working exist and can be implemented with relative ease

Could Have

- Benefits can be achieved without this
- Will not be included at this time but may be included at a later point

Won't Have

By setting out all of the work needed for successful change, more educated decisions can be taken on the volume, skill or functionality of the resources required, so availability of the right resources can be planned, avoiding last minute and often costly purchases. This understanding of the scale of the work also enables those providing the funding to understand the total cost of the change and to use this information when deciding on the viability of the change by comparing total costs against likely business value. It helps to prevent authorization of change initiatives that cannot create sufficient benefits to match all of the costs involved in the change.

Too often, barely viable changes are undertaken because the true cost of all the resources involved and the effects of disruption to business as usual have not been considered. These costs are harder to avoid when there is a detailed roadmap as it is easier to see what needs to be done and how many people this is likely to affect, which often forces a debate on how business as usual can be maintained if so many people are involved in the change effort. This is a vital debate because it is business as usual that funds the investment in the change, and if service levels fall and therefore revenue falls during a period of change then this must be included in the costs of change, which can severely impact the viability of the change idea.

This more rigorous approach to evaluating change ensures that only the strongest initiatives are given the go ahead, which can reduce the number of changes taking place at any one time. This in turn reduces the level of disruption within the organization as a whole.

Another advantage of having a roadmap is that time is not wasted at the start of each change initiative in deciding how it will be managed or what activities need to take place. A quick reference to your roadmap provides you with all of this information, which can save many days of meetings and discussions on how to proceed. This reduction of time at the start is replicated throughout the change as when there is uncertainty about what to do next, or why a certain activity is needed, the roadmap provides the explanation of what to do and how the activity fits with the other activities in the life of the change.

Case example

A team of database administrators undertook lots of change initiatives every year. They regularly designed new databases, initiated data cleansing projects and devised new reporting mechanisms for their customers. As they began work on each of these changes, they held meetings with all of those involved, discussed ideas for how the work would start, drew lots of process maps and project plans for how this would proceed and ate lots of pastries and cakes at every meeting they held! All of these discussions took several days and as it usually involved four or five people, it totalled several weeks' worth of lost effort. By devising a common roadmap of change activities, they were able to move their debate from what they had to do to how they were going to do it and to get to the creative (and more fun) part of their work completed earlier in the cycle. They could still have meetings with lots of cakes and pastries but now they were creating the solution, not arguing about how to plan the work.

This reduction in wasted time enables the lifecycle of the change to be reduced, which enables the benefits to be realized earlier. All of this means that the change initiative can start paying back its costs earlier than expected, which leads to an earlier break-even point.

Improvement in the quality of outcome

The quality of the change initiative can be improved through the use of a roadmap as all of the activities needed for its successful management have been pre-defined, therefore vital steps are less likely to be forgotten.

As the roadmap shows how each activity is connected to other activities later in the lifecycle it reduces the amount of discussion or argument about why each activity is needed. Outcomes and outputs that can be expected throughout the change are identified, which makes it easier to assure the quality of the work being done and enables those involved to manage the expectations of those impacted.

As the work is clearly described it is easier to assess the skills needed to carry out the work, increasing the chances that the most appropriate resources will be assigned to each of the tasks. Where there is a shortfall in the skills available, educated decisions can be taken about the level of support that should be given to the less skilled or experienced resources that are available.

Using the roadmap

The roadmap outlined in this chapter is formed of two elements to identify and control all of the activities needed to successfully implement agile change:

1) iterations – breaking your change into a series of smaller pieces of work that can be carried out one after the other until a new 'business as usual' has been created;

2) processes – bringing together the activities needed to achieve an important aspect of the change into processes that when joined together define the chain of events from initial idea to successful implementation.

The roadmap sets out what to do but not how to do it, as these skills and techniques are explained in subsequent chapters of this book. The three main aims of your roadmap must be to ensure that:

- you are clear what the scope and objectives of your change are and how it fits into the bigger picture of what your organization is trying to achieve strategically (business need);

- you have the ability to form productive relationships (relationships);

- you have created an environment that supports change (environment).

Tailoring the roadmap to meet your needs

The roadmap described in this chapter and the appendices contains a comprehensive set of information that has been designed to be used on any type of transformational change. When you are managing your own change you will need to tailor its contents to be relevant to your change by considering the following factors.

1. Scope, expected duration and scale of involvement by others in your change

Greater formality in what is done and how it is done is often required the more people that are involved in the change. If you don't write things down then it will be very difficult for all those participating to know what has already happened, what the results were and what still needs to be achieved.

When a small number of people are involved there is less need to document things as information can be exchanged through discussions and conversations where it is easier to include everyone and keep everyone informed.

For changes that take place over a very short period there is often limited time to document what is happening as people are too busy doing the work. Also, there is less chance that people will forget why certain decisions were taken over a shorter time period.

If the scope is narrow and clearly defined, there is less need to review lots of options for how the change will be implemented and decisions can be taken without reference to lots of research about the possible impacts.

2. The level of central control exercised in your organization

For those organizations with a hierarchical structure that requires decisions to be escalated to the relevant level of seniority, you will require closer adherence to each step of the roadmap as each individual in the chain of command can review and endorse the information before sending it their superiors for approval.

In more democratic organizations where decisions are taken close to where the changes are taking place there may be less need to follow a formal lifecycle of activities and whilst certain activities and documents in the roadmap might be helpful, much of it will be discarded in favour of flexibility and responsiveness.

3. Terminology and other methods and approaches

The roadmap will only be used if it can be easily integrated with how you work. Rename the steps and adapt the order of the activities to fit the specialist needs of your work, your corporate culture and the terminology and naming conventions used in your organization.

Successful change needs the participation of everyone who is impacted by it, so make sure that the words that you use are accessible to everyone, and are not specialist terms that those who do not have a strong project management or organizational design background will not understand.

Case example

A project management team working in a video production company had the task of designing a change management approach. They wanted to use names for their processes that included concept, design, development and implementation; however, when the sponsor saw the direction they were moving in she suggested that many of the administrators and call centre staff would not be familiar with this language. As a result of her feedback the team came up with a fun and easy-to-understand approach, which replaced their original process names with: 'Let's decide how we are going to improve things'; 'Ideasfest'; 'Let's get moving' and 'Wow, we have made a real difference'. Their final model reflected this fun, jokey language into every document and activity and has led to some really great visuals for posters and the website for their change approach.

Points to consider

Is there a high degree of central control in your organization? What effect will this level of control have on your use of the roadmap?

Structure of the roadmap

The roadmap takes account of the following points, as shown in Figure 3.3:

- expected timeframe for the change initiative;
- allocation of the available time to the iterations;
- description of the expected outcome for each iteration;
- definition of the processes used in each iteration.

Figure 3.3 Elements of the roadmap

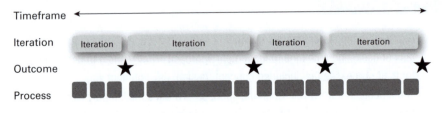

The purpose of using the roadmap is to deliver change throughout the lifecycle, not wait until the end when all aspects of the change have been created before implementing them as one complete set of changes. Every process and every iteration must deliver change, ie create the change and deploy it into the business environment so that it starts to become embedded as the new business as usual.

This emphasis on delivery must be reflected in the progress reporting that contributes to the information flow between all of those involved in the change. Progress reporting should describe what has been achieved and not what has been done. In other words it should not describe how busy everyone is – I think we have enough experience to know that everyone is busy! Reporting on busyness can be dangerous, as it gives the impression of progress when in fact there has been a lot of activity but not necessarily any progress.

Progress reporting should describe:

- what the outcomes and outputs are from each process;

- how much of this work relates to the minimum, must have change elements, and how much is part of the should have or could have elements of change;

- what the results of these outputs and outcomes are, ie do they meet their acceptance criteria, have they been deployed and have they led to improvements in the working environment which are now realizing benefits.

> **Points to consider**
>
> Create your high level overview of your roadmap by:
>
> - reviewing the scope and deciding on the number of iterations needed;
> - dividing the expected timeframe for your change into a number of weeks to be used for each iteration.

Timeframe

Why the timeframe is important

The roadmap is an effective tool for ensuring that the change is delivered by an agreed date, which is an important aspect of implementing change in an agile way. Whilst the timeframe is fixed, what is actually delivered remains flexible throughout the life of the change.

This is because it is not possible to predict in detail what will be involved in the change because of the evolving nature of the change. To be effective, the new ways of working must be capable of evolving to meet the needs of the environment, and the feedback from those implementing and being impacted by the changes.

An agreed deadline helps those affected by the change to plan when they will become involved and what arrangements they need to make to keep on top of their day-to-day work, and to explain the changes to those that rely on them.

This agile approach minimizes the disruption because whatever the scale of the changes, at least those affected know when they are going to take place. This is easier to manage than being told exactly what is going to change, but not knowing with any certainty when these changes will be ready for implementation.

Guaranteeing when the changes will be ready is also an effective way of controlling the costs of a change initiative. The majority of the costs of change are the human costs. For every extra day spent on the change, there is the cost of the salary of those involved, and the loss of productivity which reduces revenue whilst people are splitting their time between their normal duties and preparing themselves to work in a new way.

In an agile approach, as much change as possible will be delivered by the agreed end date, but the end date will not be extended, to prevent additional effort being expended to perfect the change with additions and amendments that people suddenly decide they cannot live without.

Those working in an agile way often explain this through the application of the Pareto theory: 20 per cent of the effort is spent creating 80 per cent of the solution, but a further 80 per cent of the effort can be spent achieving the last 20 per cent of the solution. So it is more efficient to create a workable solution that is 80 per cent complete than to wait until the solution is 100 per cent perfect.

I would add that in many cases the last 20 per cent of the solution is not worth waiting for, as a fast paced environment means that many of these ideas will be stale and no longer needed by the time they are delivered.

How is time allocated to the change initiative?

To ensure time is used effectively, it is allocated as follows:

- timeframe for the whole change initiative, often driven by a deadline date that meets the needs of the business;

- timeframe for the whole iteration, where the total timeframe is divided up across the required number of iterations (see the Iterations section on pages 42–45 for further explanation);

- timeframe for each of the three processes that must be carried out in every iteration (see the Processes section on pages 46–50 for further explanation);

- timeframe for individual timeboxes, which are concentrated periods of time during which the team focus on creating one element of the change.

In order to manage the expectations of those involved and ensure that the necessary resources are available when needed, a timeframe for making the changes must be agreed with the business. This will be used to create a change plan that divides this timeframe into the expected number of iterations and defines their expected outcomes.

All of the detailed changes cannot be predicted this early but some information will be needed for the business to understand how it will be affected and how it will need to prepare customers, suppliers and staff for the change.

Figure 3.4 Timeframe across the change lifecycle

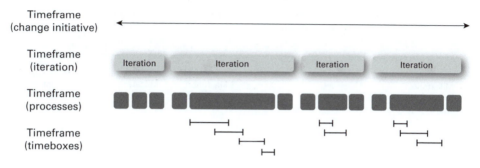

For example, if the change over the next six months is to move to a new expenses tracking system which has already been selected, then the change management plan defines at a high level how these six months will be used (Figure 3.5).

- Iteration 1 – not always shown on the change management plan as it is during this iteration that the plan is created. Some people include Iteration 1 for completeness and to show where some of the timeframe has already been used. In this case we will assume two weeks was devoted to the definition, scoping and planning of the change.

- Iteration 2 – five weeks to plan how data will be transferred to the new system and the identification of which business processes will need to be reworked.

- Iteration 3 – eight weeks to transfer the data, test out the results and create new expenses procedures and the training and support needed to deploy them.

- Iteration 4 – four weeks for the system to be activated across the first wave of departments and functions chosen to use it.

- Iteration 5 – six weeks for the system to be activated in all remaining departments and functions.

How to decide on a suitable timeframe

Deciding on a suitable timeframe should be driven by the needs of your business: internal deadlines and market-driven deadlines.

Figure 3.5 Timeframe example

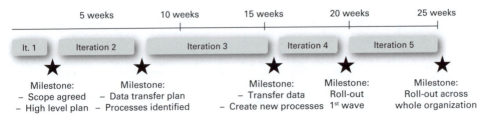

Internal deadlines are the dates by which processes must be stable and staff able to operate at full capacity. These dates derive from planned events in the business for which the changes must be in place, eg expected busy periods, known holiday periods, scheduled company announcements etc.

In some organizations, these internal deadlines create 'no go' time periods when change cannot take place (Figure 3.6). A travel company, for example, that knows that its busiest time of the year for sending out brochures and taking bookings is mid-January to mid-April. During this time they do not permit any changes to systems or processes as they believe it would pose too great a risk to their ability to deliver exceptional service and maximize holiday bookings. Similarly, they do not encourage change during August and December when a high proportion of staff take annual leave.

Figure 3.6 No go example

Jan	Feb	Mar	Apr	May	Jun	Jul	Aug	Sep	Oct	Nov	Dec

Similarly, in the Middle East it is important to avoid implementation of change during national and religious holidays as well as during the hottest months of the year when many ex pats return home.

Market-driven dates are those by when new ways of working would most usefully be in place to take advantage of customer demand for new products and services or to meet compliance dates for new regulations. For example, toy retailers need to have their marketing campaigns ready for the release date of cartoon films which create demand for toy versions of the characters.

An important market-driven date that affects universities and colleges is the new academic year. Students and staff expect new ways of working to be in place from September, as they do not want disruption once courses have begun. Any changes affecting the syllabus, the timetabling of courses and the administration of the college not implemented by this date are of little value as the ways of working in place at the start of the academic year must remain in place until the end of that year. It is possible that some changes can be implemented over the holiday period at the end of the first term or semester but in this situation the benefits of all staff and students using new systems and procedures from day one of the year will be lost.

How does the change initiative keep within the timeframe?

In an agile change, all of the change ideas are evaluated for their importance to delivering the required business value and are prioritized according to their contribution to the realization of benefits.

Exactly what will be included in the change will be prioritized according to the MoSCoW technique (also explained in Chapter 5), which assigns one of four prioritizations to each element of the change:

- must have;
- should have;
- could have;
- won't have this time.

The MoSCoW technique is used to decide what must be done, what should be done, what could be done and what will not be included in this change.

This prioritization takes place for the change as a whole, and subsequently the must, should and could items are broken down into more specific changes. Each of these are then prioritized for the iteration in which they are created. Finally, each of the specific change ideas is prioritized again to establish the order of work in a specific timebox. A timebox is a specific period of time, often only a few weeks, during which the change team are focused on making the required changes.

MoSCoW is an effective tool for managing time because it clearly establishes what work must be done first, and what work will be done if there is
any time remaining. If things take longer to create than had been antici-
pated, then all effort will be dedicated to creating the must have changes,
and should have and could have changes will not be addressed. The tool
enables those developing the changes to promise to those impacted by the
change that at least a minimum amount of change will be delivered by the
agreed deadline. This minimum amount of change, ie the must have requirements, is sufficient to make the change a reality for the users, and whilst they
might have preferred to receive the should have requirements as well, these
will be addressed by the subsequent iteration(s). If things are going well,
and the work is going according to plan then once the must have changes
have been created, time will be spent first in the should have items and then
in the could have items.

Case example

Eric is a strategic change consultant and works for a European telecoms
company that has adopted an agile approach to implementing change,
including the use of the MoSCoW technique. He believes that MoSCoW has
created a level of trust between his change team and the business that they
serve. Those affected by the changes know that his team will deliver some
change on the agreed date, even if they do not get everything that was
expected. Before he adopted MoSCoW Eric and his team would often run late
even on simple projects because of the pressure to perfect what they were
delivering, by including more and more requirements. Using MoSCoW, the
business has accepted the idea of a minimum delivery (must have items only)
on the agreed date, with the possibility of an enhanced delivery (which
includes should and some could) if the work has gone well. It's a better
working environment because the team are not accused of late delivery by
angry users and the business doesn't feel they have let their customers down
by promising them an upgrade that isn't delivered when expected.

To ensure that at least the must have items will be delivered (and hopefully to allow enough time for the should have and the could have items to be included) only 60 per cent of the timeframe will be given over to the must have items. This means that if there are problems, there is still another 40 per cent of the time that can be spent on them before running out of time. 40 per cent is a huge amount of contingency so this is how those leading the change can give such a high degree of certainty that they will meet the agreed deadline.

The best way to explain this approach is to work through an example. As part of the move to a new building it has been decided that a customer meeting area will be included in the floor plan. This is an area where members of the sales team can meet informally with customers who arrive at the office. They will be able to offer them hospitality in the form of drinks and snacks via a dedicated catering service, can sit in an informal environment to have a chat and can also show them product demonstrations in a specially created 'simulation pod' where they can experience the latest products.

The creation of the customer meeting area is a must have for the office move change initiative. However, it can be broken down into smaller, more specific changes so that each of them can be assigned their own priority according to the business value provided. The informal seating area is a must have, but the creation of a simulation pod is a should have. The provision of drinks and snacks is a could have because there is a coffee shop next door to the office where the sales team can get the necessary drinks if needed.

The tables and chairs in the informal seating area are a must have but other furniture requirements such as pictures on the wall and stands for holding brochures and other sales literature are a could have.

Points to consider

Are there any times during the next calendar year when implementing change in your area of the business would cause an unacceptable level of disruption?

Iterations

Iterations provide an explanation of how this timeframe will be used, by dividing the change into a series of outcomes, each of which is delivered by an iteration. These outcomes are an element of the overall change, comprising a number of must, should and could have aspects, created in accordance with the priority based on their ability to realize benefits and meet business need. The use of iterations enables the scope of the change to be divided up into sections, with the option to stop the change after completion of any of the sections.

In using an agile approach we accept that the change will evolve over time, and that all of the changes cannot be planned in detail at the start. We will achieve our change through the repeated delivery of small changes that when taken together will create a new working environment. As each change is delivered to the users, we go back and repeat the steps again, to deliver further changes and enhancements to the changes already completed.

To reflect the repeatable nature of our change activities, we can divide the change into iterations (Figure 3.7). This is similar to project and programme management methods that divide the project lifecycle into stages or tranches, which are only completed once all of the activities have been undertaken.

Figure 3.7 Iterations of the change

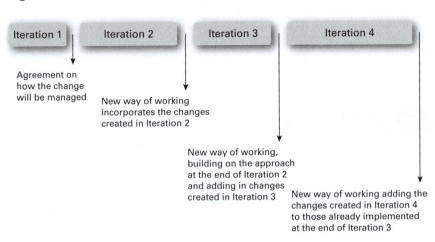

Number of iterations

The number of iterations needed to implement your change will depend upon:

- The amount of time available for the change, driven by internal or market-driven deadlines.

- The likely concentration period of those involved in the change, as each iteration should last only as long as people can reasonably remain focused on the tasks.

- The type of work involved – some changes will take longer to develop than others and it is important that the duration of the iterations reflects this. There is no need for each iteration to be the same length of time, so long as the outcome expected from the iteration aligns to the amount of time the iteration is expected to last.

- The expected complexity of the change – it is easier to keep people focused on what needs to be done if the change can be made as simple as possible. Try to group changes to similar or related areas of work together in one iteration and clarify the scope of the iteration so everyone knows what should be in place by the time it ends so that there is no confusion about what is required.

- The amount of feedback given by the users when presented with each element of the change and which will need to be incorporated in subsequent iterations.

- The number of unexpected and unplanned outcomes from the change that will need to be reacted to in subsequent iterations.

Whatever the scale of the change you are involved in, you will need to divide your work into a minimum of two iterations: the first iteration is used for assessing the impact of the change, understanding its size and scope and using this information to understand the expected work involved and how it will be divided up into further iterations; and the second iteration is where the work is done and the changes are made.

For large or complex changes there will be third, fourth, fifth iterations and so on until the change is completed. However, in an agile environment we must be prepared to end the change initiative as soon as it has created enough change to deliver the necessary benefits. This is why the first iteration should be short, as an extended period of planning to define the outcome of multiple iterations would be a waste of time if the change is halted after iteration two or three.

Aligning the iterations

An important consideration for how your change is implemented is to decide whether all work in an iteration must be completed before starting the next iteration or if the activities involved in realizing the benefits can take place whilst the subsequent iteration commences.

Figure 3.8 Sequential iterations

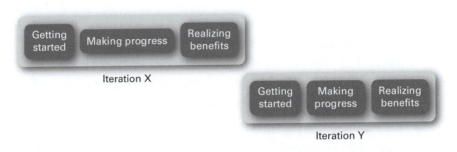

In Figure 3.8 Iteration Y does not begin until all of the activities in realizing benefits from Iteration X, ie dismantle/deploy and celebrate, have been carried out. The figure also reminds us that iterations are not necessarily of the same length, and the amount of time needed for Iteration Y is less than for Iteration X.

Figure 3.9 Overlapping iterations

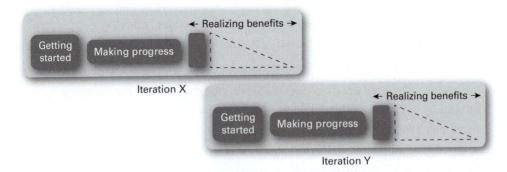

In Figure 3.9 Iteration Y begins once the deployment activities in realizing benefits in Iteration X have been completed and before the dismantling of the old world and celebrating of the new has been completed. This is because many of the activities involved in measuring the benefits and celebrating the achievements take place over an extended timeframe, likely to be a minimum of several months. In this diagram this 'long tail' is shown as a triangle where the effort involved decreases over time.

Waiting for the results of one iteration to become fully embedded before starting work on the next iteration might not be practical, as it would extend the total duration of the change past an acceptable date for the business. However, a balance must be achieved between deploying the change and getting reactions from this deployment (which form additional requirements for the next iteration) and keeping momentum for the change by moving into the next iteration as swiftly as possible.

Points to consider

Identify how many key deliverables your change is likely to deliver and in what order they will become available. Now see if you can map these to two or three iterations spanning the time available for your change.

How will your change work in practice? Can you wait until all aspects of realizing benefits have been completed before commencing work on the next iteration or would beginning the next iteration straight after deployment be more effective?

Outcomes

For each iteration it is important to specify the outcome. An outcome is the desired result from carrying out all of the activities and producing the outputs. The desired result can be expressed in terms of tangible, physical achievements, eg all customer enquiries receive an e-mail acknowledgement, or it can be a behavioural change, eg we consider the customer impact of every activity we carry out. These outcomes will be different depending on where in the lifecycle of the change they are being created, ie which iteration produces them.

The first iteration has a different outcome to all the other iterations. This is because the first iteration is used for assessing the impact of the overall change and specifying the business need and high level requirements. This information enables those leading the change to identify how many subsequent iterations there will be. Each of these subsequent iterations delivers specific aspects of the change.

The outcome for the second and subsequent iterations will be driven by the business need. Ideally each iteration will deliver an outcome that is capable of generating benefits as these will:

- Generate motivation to continue the change through further iterations as those involved realize that the change has delivered a tangible positive effect on how work is undertaken.

- Create improvements in the business environment that will make it easier to apply further changes. For example, streamlining processes makes it easier to introduce new systems as there are fewer processes to amend to reflect use of the new system.

- Reduce costs or increase revenue that will help fund subsequent changes. By delivering beneficial outcomes at the end of every iteration, the return on investment is increased as benefits are experienced earlier in the lifecycle and begin the process of paying back the costs earlier, shortening the amount of time taken for the change to break even.

Processes

To achieve the outcome of each iteration, it is important to follow an agreed set of processes that define the work, carry out the change activities and measure their achievements. Processes group together the activities needed to progress through each iteration, making sure that there is a consistency to how the change is developed and delivered, irrespective of the specialist work involved.

To keep things simple there are three processes that are repeated for each iteration:

- Getting started – this process defines and plans the work that will take place in the iteration. Those participating in the change will decide what the iteration is expected to achieve, identify what work is required and how this will be allocated across the available resources.

- Making progress – this process creates the changes. This is the most significant part of the iteration, to which most time and resources are dedicated because it is where the new ways of working are designed and tested.

- Realizing benefits – this process deploys the changes into the live business environment and checks that the desired benefits are being generated.

To contribute to the control of the change, these processes should each be allocated a proportion of the time allowed for the whole of the iteration. This ensures that time will be available for each of the three activities, and that an activity is not allowed to overrun at the expense of the time given to the subsequent activities.

For example, to remain aligned to agile principles, it is important that the research and planning associated with getting started does not dominate the iteration. This process should be swift, providing sufficient information for changes to be developed. The majority of the iteration must be dedicated to making the changes and then deploying them to create the new working environment. For this reason, it is sensible to set the following guidelines:

- getting started – 10–20 per cent of the timeframe for the iteration;
- making progress – 60 per cent of the timeframe for the iteration;
- realizing benefits – 10–20 per cent of the timeframe for the iteration.

Figure 3.10 Processes within an iteration

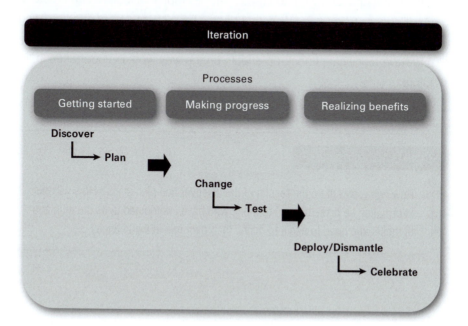

Getting started

Getting started takes place at the beginning of every iteration, and establishes what needs to be done. It is formed of two activities:

1 Discover – this is about understanding what has been achieved so far, what remains to be done and what successful completion of this iteration will contribute to the overall change. It requires ideas generation and innovative thinking to define how work will be conducted in the future and identify what needs to be in place to make this a reality.

2 Plan – in the plan step, those involved decide what actions need to be taken to develop the ideas generated in the discover step. They will be prioritizing them using their understanding of the benefits that the change must deliver and the business need that must be met by the change. Those involved will then decide how to allocate the work amongst each other. This planning also involves the creation of acceptance criteria against which the changes can be evaluated prior to being implemented.

It is important to define 'what good looks like' before any of the work is done so that changes are assessed against objective criteria. Without these acceptance criteria, there is a risk that changes will be evaluated by emotional factors which include the amount of effort involved, who was involved or how difficult the changes were to create. These emotional factors can create an unwillingness to leave out work that people have spent a lot of effort creating. This can affect the integrity of the change, as even one unnecessary change can have significant knock-on effects on the way work is undertaken in the future.

Points to consider

How will you capture the results of the discover and plan steps? How will this information be disseminated to those who have contributed to its creation and to those who need to use it to define their own role in the change?

Making progress

Making progress is where the work is created according to the priority agreed and the resources specified in the plan activity. It is formed of two activities:

1 Change – innovation in how tasks are undertaken to meet the business need. These changes must address: creating the new ways of working, ie being specific about how work will be carried out, who will be responsible, what information, systems and infrastructure will be used and how it will be used; and creating the conditions for operational use, ie all of the activities needed to make the business environment ready for the change, which might include notifications to customers, suppliers and/or regulators, training of staff, arranging for the delivery or removal of new equipment etc.

These two activities must be considered together because creating change in isolation from the activities needed to deploy it masks the total work involved and may lead to an over-commitment of resources as those who have finished creating new ways of working might be expected to move onto the next iteration without having had the time to create the conditions for operational use. Failure to acknowledge that both of these aspects are required can also give an unrealistic expectation of the work that can be achieved in the timeframe set for the iteration, as lots of change can be created if the conditions for its use are not addressed.

2 Test – this is where the changes are reviewed against the acceptance criteria and any non-conformances are addressed. It is very important to test the workability of each change as early as possible, before it forms part of a bigger change – the earlier problems are found, the cheaper they are to rectify. It is much easier to fix an individual element of the change than redesign an entire process later in the change initiative or when the change has been implemented and been found not to work.

Realizing benefits

Realizing benefits is formed of two activities:

1 Dismantle/Deploy – this is the point at which changes are incorporated into the live business environment. If users need to be shown how to operate the new procedures or systems then this should be completed as part of this process. Dismantle is where old ways of working are removed so that costs are not duplicated by maintaining obsolete processes, systems or structures, and people are not tempted to return to the old ways of working.

2 Celebrate is an important step in generating the motivation for continual change. Celebration comes from congratulating people on the effort they have made and publicizing the evidence of what has been achieved by measuring the benefits.

Part 2: Applying the roadmap to your change

In this next section we look specifically at what you need to do and what information is involved in delivering your change. As we mentioned earlier in this chapter, when discussing tailoring, it is recommended that you name the documents used in your roadmap to fit with the terminology and culture of your organization. So this section does not contain document templates but indicates the type of information you will need to define, explains why this is important and provides criteria to be able to assess that the information you are generating is relevant and complete.

For more guidance on formally capturing information about your change go to Appendix 2: Change management documents (page 241).

Iteration 1

The outcome of this first iteration is a common understanding of what the change is expected to achieve by all those involved in making it a reality and a description of how the change will be managed.

This iteration is a one off. It is different to all subsequent iterations because it creates the outputs needed to manage the change and does not create any specialist aspects of the change. Managing the change requires coordination of the change activities and application of the governance framework to ensure that decisions are made by appropriately empowered individuals.

As the detailed understanding of what needs to change will evolve throughout the lifecycle of the change this iteration should be kept short as the majority of the effort must be given to creating and implementing the changes. An agile approach does not support detailed planning of the unknown but is more flexible, creating enough structure to clarify what is to be done, but recognizing the details will only be available at the point that the work is done. Time should not be spent estimating what is to be done and how long it will take based on untested assumptions of what is needed and how skilled the resources are (and therefore how productive) and how long it will take them.

Iteration 1 is an important step in creating the necessary trust between all those involved in the change. Trust is based on doing what you say you are going to do so step 1 is to say what you are going to do, then build in steps to correct the course of your communication from intended meaning to what is actually heard. Do this little and often before misinterpretations become entrenched.

Iteration 1 must be authorized by the change sponsor, because even if no money is spent in developing the outputs from this iteration (see Appendix 1) the time of those involved that could still have been devoted to business as usual has been redirected to the change initiative.

The activities carried out in this iteration are:

Getting started

Figure 3.11 Processes within getting started

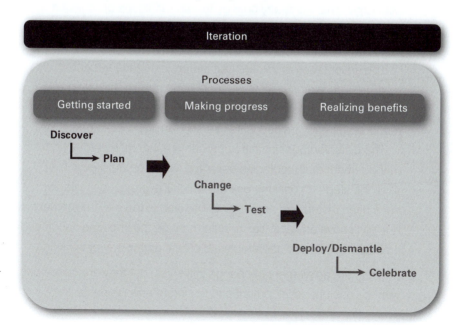

Discover

This is the research phase, during which all available information about the drivers for the change, its expected benefits and those who have requested it is gathered and reviewed. This will help to establish the scale of the change which will affect how formally it is to be managed. Questions to ask at this point include:

- Are the benefits expected to be realized internally or will they also be experienced by external parties (customers and/or suppliers)?
- Are the expected benefits of interest to those who audit or legislate your industry?
- Are the internal benefits cross-functional or are they specific to one business function?

Answers to these questions will help you consider who to involve in the plan activity. Please see Chapter 4: Business need, for more information on this.

One of the questions to ask is, if there is an infrastructure already in place to manage projects, how should this be incorporated into managing the change initiative? Broadly speaking, there are two schools of thought:

1 Projects deliver change by creating the new products, services, processes and systems that enable the organization to work differently. Therefore, any change initiative is a type of project and so it should be managed according to the project management methodology already in operation within your organization.

The advantages of this are that the project management methodology already exists, so there is no need to adopt a new change management roadmap, and that there are likely to be resources already trained in its use and familiar with its operation.

The disadvantages of this approach are that many project management methodologies cover the development lifecycle, ie all of the steps up until the point at which the project deliverables have been tested and are ready to be used in the live environment, but don't have any activities to help manage the implementation and embedding of these deliverables to create a new way of working.

2 Projects are an element of change initiatives, but they are concerned with the design, development and testing of new products and

services, and do not include the transformation of the organization to prepare for their use.

The advantages of this are that the project remains focused on creating the deliverables and does not get distracted by all of the activities needed to 'sell' the benefits of working in new ways to all those who will need to work differently in order to use the project deliverables.

The disadvantages of this are that projects are not aligned to the overall business changes needed to realize the benefits, and that whilst they deliver project outputs on time, on budget and to the required level of quality, they have not incorporated elements that will assist in their implementation.

By the end of this first iteration, the approach to managing projects and managing the change that they create will need to have been agreed.

Another aspect of the discover activity is understanding the wider context of the change. Are these changes being made in isolation from other initiatives or do they form an integral part of an organization-wide transformation? If they are part of a wider programme of change activities, is there a central governance or control function? For example, in some organizations, there is a central function (variously called a project, programme or portfolio office, change management office or strategy office) that uses the strategic objectives to identify and plan all projects and change initiatives, and will ask all those involved to provide progress reports so that what has been achieved can be understood in the context of all other initiatives.

It will be important to discover how much autonomy you have for managing the change as this will affect the formality of your documentation and the number of constraints that you are operating under. Important factors to consider are:

- Is there a direct relationship between yourself and the change sponsor or do you have to work through an intermediary, eg your line manager or a programme or change office?

- Can you rely on the sponsor to provide you with information about other, related initiatives taking place in the organization or do you need to source this information for yourself?

- Are there any information sharing forums already set up in your organization, eg user groups or enterprise social media, which you can engage with to explain the changes you are making?

Mark works as a project manager in a financial services organization where there is very little informal discussion of what is happening elsewhere in the organization. After finding that those whose jobs were being impacted by his projects were also implementing changes from other projects and initiatives that he knew nothing about he began to get frustrated. This extra work often caused delays to his 'go-live' date and sometimes made his project deliverables obsolete before they had even been used because process changes removed the need for them. As a result he has set up a 'Monthly Mingle' which happens on a Thursday lunchtime. Food is provided and there is always a talk from one of the senior managers to explain an aspect of strategy, followed by an informal discussion of who is doing what. These sessions have become so popular they are now videoed, with the video added to the company intranet. The forum enabled Mark and his colleagues to meet project managers from other areas of the business that have the same internal customers and they now meet regularly to align their plans and agree a series of implementation dates that ensures that multiple changes do not take place at the same time.

Plan

The information from the discover activity is used to plan what needs to be created in order to manage the change. If the organization's project management methodology is to be applied then this will specify the documents to be created in the making progress activity. Alternatively, those involved will define their own information needs based on their tailoring of this and other change management roadmaps and approaches.

Whatever the information needs, the plan activity is where the work of creating, reviewing and authorizing the management approach will be assigned to the available resources.

Creating documents is appropriate if you are implementing change across a large group of people, but if you are working with a few close colleagues then it is better to scale these documents appropriately, whilst making sure you provide information for each of the suggested headings.

Making progress

Figure 3.12 Processes within making progress

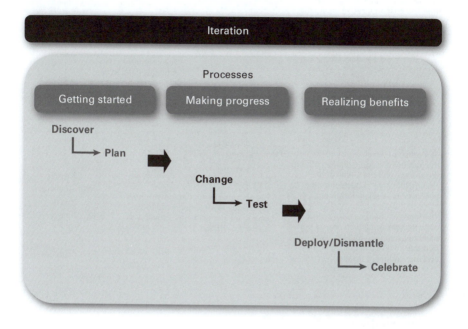

The changes created in this first iteration are the development of the change roadmap, either as a new approach or an agreement to apply an existing approach.

The outputs created in making progress will be whatever is needed to:

- explain the proposed changes to others;
- prove the validity and necessity of the change;
- define the governance structure;
- ensure those involved in the change know what work needs to be completed and when;
- keep everyone informed of progress, issues and risks.

Each of these outputs is connected to the others (Figure 3.13).

Figure 3.13 Outputs created in Iteration 1

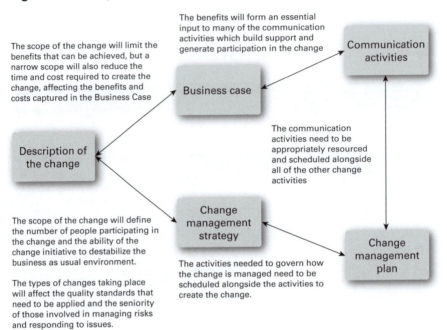

The scope of the change will limit the benefits that can be achieved, but a narrow scope will also reduce the time and cost required to create the change, affecting the benefits and costs captured in the Business Case

The benefits will form an essential input to many of the communication activities which build support and generate participation in the change

The communication activities need to be appropriately resourced and scheduled alongside all of the other change activities

The scope of the change will define the number of people participating in the change and the ability of the change initiative to destabilize the business as usual environment.

The types of changes taking place will affect the quality standards that need to be applied and the seniority of those involved in managing risks and responding to issues.

The activities needed to govern how the change is managed need to be scheduled alongside the activities to create the change.

Description of the change

The purpose of the description of the change is to create an understanding of what will be different in the future. It is reviewed at the start of each iteration, acting as an important source of reference for what is required and helping to prioritize the work based on the intended scope and expected deliverables of the change. It includes:

- vision;
- scope and exclusions;
- expected deliverables;
- assumptions and constraints;
- links with other work.

One of the techniques that can help to describe the change is to create a model or a prototype. The model can bring the change to life in a way that a document cannot as it is a tangible, physical manifestation of the change that those involved in the change can experience. For example, redesigning processes can be modelled using sticky notes on a wall, with each sticky note summarizing each of the steps in the process. This immediately conveys the length of the process, the inputs to it and the outputs from it and enables those reviewing it to understand where they would be involved and what happens before and after their involvement.

If this early demonstration of the likely changes to the process is accepted by those impacted then the detailed work can begin. It also provides an opportunity for those impacted to generate more ideas about what needs to be included in the change, or what should be left out. In my experience these early demonstrations of tangible progress with the change reduce the demand for some of the more outlandish requirements. This is because once the change has been experienced, it generates ideas about keeping things simple and easy to operate.

I use a lot of modelling to demonstrate possible changes before they are formally included in the scope of the overall change and am always amazed by the volume and quality of the information that I get back. One of the most valuable aspects to modelling is how it changes the conversation about change from something nebulous that might happen in the future to some-thing real that is happening now. I find this shift in perspective really engages those impacted and helps them to see what preparations they need to start making to get ready for change.

Business case

The purpose of the business case is to demonstrate why the change is needed and how it will deliver improvements to market position and internal capability over and above what exist today. In common with the change description, it is reviewed at the start of each iteration to understand what benefits should be delivered, which in turn affects decisions on the priority of change ideas. It contains the following elements:

- benefits;
- risks;
- costs.

Creating this document forms an important step in helping everyone involved in the change to identify for themselves why they think the change is important. As we see in later chapters, people have a different context and a different perspective on change based on their personality type, their previous experience of change and the type of change that is taking place. Try to establish if there really is a problem with the current way of working, and ask people to articulate what these issues are, and describe the difficulties that they are experiencing. Use the description of the change to create a compelling future state in which people can see a role for themselves and can instinctively see how the future would be an improvement on the present and make sure that the change management plan sets out a workable approach that appears practical and achievable so that people can believe the change will be achieved and will not be a waste of their effort.

Change management strategy

The purpose of the change management strategy is to explain how all of the change activities will be coordinated and managed. As the change evolves different people will become involved at different times so the change management strategy acts as a rapid induction, providing guidance on the governance of the change initiative and specific aspects of its day-to-day management including progress reporting and the control of risks and issues. It contains the following elements:

- organization structure;
- how risks and issues are escalated;
- balance of change activities with 'business as usual';
- how quality of the work is checked;
- how progress is to be tracked and reported.

Change management plan

The purpose of the change management plan is to define how the overall timeframe for the change will be divided across the various iterations to create the specialist elements of the change, and how this work is supported by activities to manage the change as a whole, outlined in the change management strategy. The key elements of the plan are:

- timeframe;
- use of the processes defined in the roadmap;
- governance;

- resources;
- workstreams;
- assumptions;
- constraints.

Communication plan

To maximize support for the change and encourage those involved to actively participate, regular and detailed information will need to be made available (Figure 3.14).

- This communication activity takes a lot of time and by identifying it early in the change you can agree with your colleagues how the work will be allocated.
- Communication is needed for two different groups: those who are changing how they work as a result of the change; and the wider stakeholder group who need to be consulted and who have important information to share but whose work will not be directly affected. The wider stakeholder group includes:

  - senior managers responsible for the analysis and planning of the organization's strategic objectives;
  - operational managers who are responsible for processes and systems that are subject to change;
  - functional managers responsible for performance management of an aspect of the organization which will be impacted by the change, eg HR responsible for staff turnover or marketing responsible for brand awareness.

Figure 3.14 Information flow

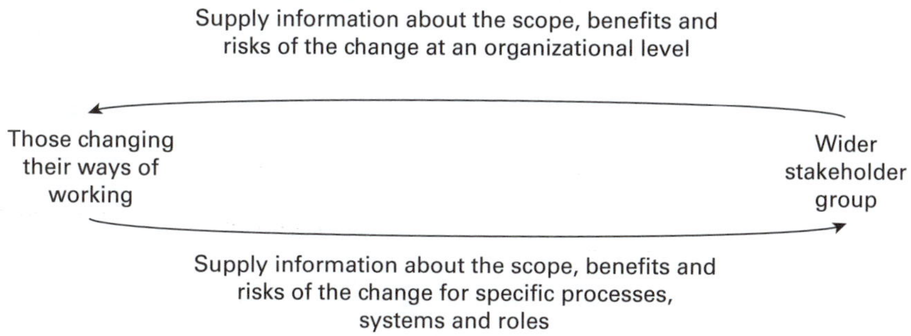

Supply information about the scope, benefits and
risks of the change at an organizational level

Those changing
their ways of
working

Wider
stakeholder
group

Supply information about the scope, benefits and
risks of the change for specific processes,
systems and roles

Figure 3.15 Summary of communication activities

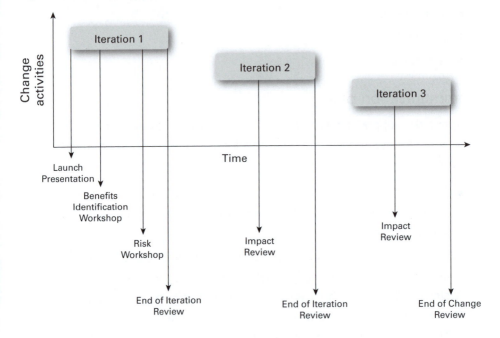

The communication plan will evolve over the life of the change into a detailed record of all the communication events. At this early point in the change, it should minimally include the most important events (Figure 3.15).

Refer to Appendix 3 for suggested agendas for each of these communication events and an explanation of the facilitated workshop technique for carrying them out.

Test   The content created in making progress will need to be reviewed by those sponsoring the change and those who will be managing it as it moves through its lifecycle. Before deploying the change framework you will need to know that those who are using them believe they meet their acceptance criteria.

Are there any other documents suggested in your organization's project management methodology or quality management system that would be appropriate for your change?

Who are the best sources of information for you to complete your description of the change?

What other communication events are needed to help manage your change?

Realizing benefits

Figure 3.16 Processes within realizing benefits

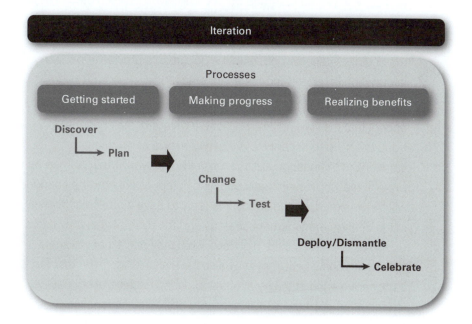

Deploy/Dismantle

As Iteration 1 comes to a close, your roadmap should be shared and explained to all those who will be involved in making change happen. It is not
necessary for everyone to know every aspect of the roadmap. Demonstrate
your respect for how busy they already are by selecting the relevant information
for each audience member, whilst making the rest of the roadmap available
for those who wish to understand it in full. For example:

- You as the change leader need to demonstrate ownership of the
  roadmap that you are going to apply to the change. This ownership
  responsibility includes making it available to all who need it and being
  open to suggestions about improvements to it. After all, the roadmap
  is a product of an agile approach to change so it should be regarded
  as an evolving solution and not a fixed and final version.

- Participants – those that will become involved in change in at least
  one of the iterations will benefit from an overview of the processes
  and activities in the roadmap but are unlikely to be interested in all of
  the detailed documentation pertaining to the governance of the
  change. As a minimum, share with them the change description and
  the business case as both of these documents provide important
  information for prioritizing the change activities.

- Change sponsor – it is difficult for those in the sponsorship role to
  accept that they will not know all of the details of the changes up
  front, but have to accept that these will evolve as each of the
  iterations of the change are successfully deployed. The roadmap can
  provide reassurance in that it contains details about how the change
  will be governed, so the sponsor is likely to have a particular interest
  in the change management strategy and the plan, so that they can
  understand at least at the high level what they can expect to see
  happening and when. They may also have an interest in the resources
  assigned to each of the iterations and during each iteration may be
  interested to see how work is allocated across the timeboxes. This is
  because their management role will require them to balance the needs
  of the change against the needs of the business as usual environment.

- Auditor – those needing to assure others that the change is being
  well managed will be particularly interested in the change

management strategy and the plan. They will not be interested in the specialist work other than to reassure themselves that the management of the change has considered the need to balance business as usual and change activities and that the deployment at the end of each iteration has been sufficiently well planned so that it will not destabilize the working environment or risk lowering levels of customer service or satisfaction.

In the case of Iteration 1, the dismantle activity can be used to create the necessary time for all those involved in the change to participate by removing any tasks, meetings, reports etc from their current day jobs that can be temporarily suspended in order to make time for change.

Celebrate

It is helpful to celebrate the creation and/or the adoption of the roadmap as it is an opportunity to thank everyone for their hard work in thinking through how change will take place. Congratulating individuals on their contribution and the ideas they have had for how change can be managed successfully will build their confidence in their ability to participate in the change and will help to develop collaborative working by creating a team environment.

Public thanks for these individuals will also draw the attention of those who have not participated so far which is another opportunity to let everyone know that change is happening. The roadmap will build confidence in the wider community as the initiative will be viewed as organized and well thought through, which will help to dispel some of the disquiet that those expecting to be impacted by it might be feeling.

How will you know that Iteration 1 has been a success?

Before leaving Iteration 1 it is important to review what it should have achieved and check that everything that should have been done has been done. This iteration is a one off, it sets the ground rules for how the change will be managed so if there are any gaps in the planning or definition of the change initiative, now is the time to fill them. Measure your satisfaction with Iteration 1 by assessing how you feel about the following aspects:

- there is a genuine feeling amongst all of those you need to work with that the change is important and achievable;

- there is common agreement amongst those working on the change about the type and amount of business value that the change will create;

- you feel confident that you have identified all those who will be impacted by the change or who will need to contribute to it and you have begun communicating with them;

- the boundaries within which the change is to be delivered have been defined and agreed with senior management including the timeframe and the minimum requirements for the change.

Iteration 2 and subsequent iterations

The outcome of Iteration 2 and all subsequent iterations are the actual changes needed to realize the benefits. The activities required are summarized in Figure 3.17.

Figure 3.17 Information created in each process

As the information created in this iteration will be specific to your change I have not included any templates. However, I do recommend that to simplify the change activities as much as possible, you do create your own templates and draft agendas for regular meetings and presentations.

Case example

A very well organized change team in a food manufacturing business put a lot of effort into creating presentation templates for announcing changes, reporting on progress and explaining new ways of working. They created formats that they all agreed on for process maps, organization structures and system maps.

The reason for all this effort was because they were used to carrying out a lot of changes to processes, and as a result found that their users don't always realize when changes were being made. However, the change team also found that they were spending a lot of time creating information that was broadly similar for many of the changes and so looked to reduce this overhead to spend more time on actually making the changes instead.

To resolve this the change team created an induction pack that they updated every month with information about each change including the background, information about the key people and processes that are involved and summaries of past presentations so that anyone joining the team can get up to speed quickly and feel a part of the team. This induction pack also includes details of any administration procedures including claiming expenses, how to fill in the Risk and Issue Logs and how to use their version control procedures.

Creating the communication information about the change is now a standard task and is a lot quicker because nothing has to be created as the templates are already available. They have had compliments about the professionalism of their material which has made them feel proud of their work.

Getting started

The activities in this process support an agile approach by empowering those involved in the change to take responsibility for their work. The team in place for this iteration will need to agree on the usefulness and appropriateness of the work by evaluating its contribution to benefits as well as its practicability and its achievability.

Those items that are identified as difficult to achieve might be categorized as 'won't have this time' to protect the team from work that has little chance of success at the expense of other changes that can be achieved and will realize benefits when the iteration is deployed.

Practicability and/or achievability is subjective and is indicated by the team's confidence in:

- their level of knowledge about the task;
- their past experience in carrying out similar tasks;
- access to expertise and support outside of the team;
- senior management interest or political support for the task;
- level of inter-connectedness with other work;
- probability that this work will lead to the need for further changes.

Discussions about practicability and achievability enable the team to agree the priority of each task, identify how they are going to approach the work and who is best suited for each task.

Discover

Ideas will be generated from all those involved in the iteration even if not everyone will be involved in the activities to develop and implement these changes.

To maximize the creativity of this step, there needs to be up-to-date progress reporting from the previous iteration and open and honest sharing of information amongst all of the participants to ensure that lessons can be learnt from the previous work and that mistakes or omissions can be addressed in this iteration. Idea generation will involve:

- reviewing feedback on the changes made in the last iteration;
- identifying new ideas based on a review of how work is carried out today;
- asking those who provide inputs or rely on outputs from the existing approach to clarify their needs;
- asking those responsible for the efficiency and accuracy of the process for their ideas;

- asking those responsible for ensuring the process is followed for their ideas.

In leading the change effort, you will need to guide those affected by the change to be creative and innovative in deciding what needs to change. Working collaboratively and facilitating discussions where ideas are explained and added to is an essential part of your role.

Active listening It's important to take the time to listen to your users, allowing them to describe and share their ideas or articulate the problems and challenges that they need to solve.

Use 'active listening', which is a technique where the listener feeds back what they have heard from the speaker, confirming their understanding and allowing the speaker to gain insight into what they have said by having it played back to them. The steps in the active listening technique are:

1 **Building rapport** – using eye contact and creating an environment that invites the speaker to begin sharing their information. This includes finding somewhere to talk where you are unlikely to be interrupted and giving the speaker your full attention, eg putting away your phone or turning away from your PC. This demonstrates that you are fully 'present', ie that the speaker has your full attention.

2 **Mirroring the information back to the speaker** – playing back the words and phrases used by the speaker to ensure you have not missed anything and giving them a chance to add any additional information. You will use phrases including 'this is what I have heard' and 'what I think you told me was . . .'. This demonstrates to the speaker that you have been listening which builds their willingness to continuing to share information with you.

3 **Interpreting what you have heard** – reflecting back the feelings you have heard and your perceptions helps the speaker acknowledge any disconnect between what they are feeling as indicated by the gestures, tone of voice, speed and volume of speaking etc and what they are saying.

4 **Encouraging the speaker to draw a conclusion** – this is when you have summarized the information shared so far and give the speaker an opportunity to summarize their ideas and articulate them as requirements for change.

Successful active listening plays back the words and phrases used by the speaker along with the emotional subtext that they gave these words. This allows the speaker to understand any disconnect between what they have said and what they really feel so that they can improve upon their ideas and create a way forward that is right for them.

To help your users create their ideas for change, encourage them to assess their current situation. For example, ask them the following questions:

- Which processes do you most enjoy and least enjoy carrying out? And why?

- Which of the processes that you carry out receives the most compliments or complaints? (ask them to give you examples of the compliments or complaints and who is making them)

- Which of the processes that you carry out involve the most or the fewest people? (ask them why they think this is the case)

- What data or information do you use the most or the least often?

- Is there any information that requires format changes before it can be used, and how long does this take? (eg re-keying information from a report into a spreadsheet)

Feedback Devising new ways of working can be a creative time but it can also be a time of great anxiety, as it is when we are faced with the reality of having to learn something new and unlearn how we currently work. Instinctively we realize that this work will take longer to complete until the new approach becomes familiar, and it is this realization that can begin an internal argument about how necessary the change is and how it would be better to hold onto the old ways of working. One technique is to break down the design of the new ways of working into small pieces of work with specific targets for achievement so that it is easier to track progress and harder to get lost.

One of the ways in which we can help people devise new ways of working is to give them constructive feedback on their ideas. Feedback is not criticism. Criticism is negative and judgemental and in many cases benefits the person giving it by making them feel superior to the person receiving it. Feedback helps the person receiving it to improve on their ideas and to identify alternative courses of action that will be more effective than what was originally planned.

When helping people to change how they work make sure the feedback focuses on the practicality, desirability or performance of the approach. Don't make it personal and don't comment on the ability of the receiver to carry out the work.

The feedback should be specific, asking questions about how the new way of working actually works, or how it connects to other pieces of work or the skills needed to carry it out. Use this as an opportunity to share stories of similar situations and the approach that you have taken or have seen others take and how this compares with what you have just been shown.

Case example

In a change programme for a local medical centre, the receptionists had decided to introduce automatic text messaging to remind patients of their appointments. When they asked me to review the processes for making patient appointments, I helped them to refine their initial idea:

- Summarize – I reflected back the process as I had heard it to check that I had not missed any facts and to demonstrate the steps that I believed had been communicated to me.

- Opinion – I took the position of a patient and I demonstrated how I felt about receiving the text message reminder. I carried out this step several times because I wanted to portray the views of as many different patient types as possible, including those that do not have a mobile phone.

- Impact – I asked the receptionists for their views on what they had heard from me and facilitated a discussion on their ideas for enhancing and changing their initial process to improve the imagined views of the patients.

- Summarize – I summarized the action plan I had heard and asked the receptionists to decide on when the actions would be taken and by whom.

Points to consider

Make a list of the questions you would ask your colleagues to help them identify their ideas for the change.

The output from this discovery step is an agreement on the scope of the iteration and an understanding of the time allocated for this iteration: the scope is agreed using the prioritized requirements list; and the time allocated is taken from the change management plan.

Plan

Prioritizing the work
If this is the first iteration to deliver changes into the live environment then you will create the prioritized requirements list. The prioritized requirements list does exactly as its title suggests. It lists each of the required changes in order or priority, beginning with the must have items and concluding with those requirements that have been identified but are not viewed as important enough to be included in the change so are categorized as won't have.

In subsequent iterations the original prioritized requirements list will be updated. The discovery step will begin with a review of what requirements remain outstanding, along with the addition of requirements that have been requested as those impacted start to understand how they will be impacted by the change. All of the requirements will be re-prioritized to provide the scope of the iteration. The scope is all must have items, followed by the should have items followed by the could have items. See Chapter 4: Business need for a further explanation of the prioritized requirements list.

The change management plan is a useful reference document because it provides a description of the high level deliverables or products expected from this iteration, which will influence the decisions on what needs to be done. It also defines how many iterations the change is expected to have which enables those involved to see how far through the work they are and what should already be in place for them to enhance as part of the evolving solution.

The Plan step should confirm the expected outputs from this iteration and prioritize them using the MoSCoW technique. The change description provides the understanding of the business need used to prioritize the work. It is important that everyone agrees and understands what the highest priority items are so that they can focus on achieving these first, with any remaining time allocated to the should have and could have items.

Allocating the work
In this plan step there will need to be agreement on how work will be managed. Once the scope of this iteration has been agreed, the work will need to be broken down into specific tasks and resources

can be allocated according to the skills required and the motivation of those involved to volunteer for the work. The majority of the work should be allocated to those who believe they are best suited to carrying it out, so they feel as motivated as possible. Any remaining tasks will have to be allocated by you in your role as change leader.

Whilst an agile approach to delivering the change requires high degrees of self-direction this is not an excuse to concentrate on the specialist work at the expense of the governance activities. It may be necessary to nominate someone to be responsible for managing issues and risks and collating the progress reporting for the whole iteration in accordance with the approach set out in the change management strategy.

Alternatively, everyone may decide to take responsibility for addressing risks and issues directly with their colleagues with progress reporting happening verbally.

Points to consider

How can you record information about who is doing what so that everyone can see who is involved and what they are doing?

Alongside the creation of the 'timebox' plan for the development of the specialist aspects of the change, an implementation plan may be created to define the work involved in realizing benefits.

Acceptance criteria   Finally, before leaving the plan activity, the criteria against which the outputs will be assessed must be defined. These will be specific to each of the specialist outputs. In some cases the acceptance criteria can be derived from externally imposed quality standards or industry norms. In other cases the key performance indicators that measure the success of the current ways of working can be adapted to apply to the new ways of working. Finally, some of the specialist work can only be assessed using subjective criteria, evaluating the satisfaction with or suitability that staff ascribe to the new ways of working. Even though these criteria are subjective they should still be defined in advance so that everyone is in agreement about what good looks like before they start work.

Allocating the time   The plan allocates the work to those involved. This might be quite informal, with people suggesting what their contribution will be and agreeing amongst themselves how the work will be allocated across the various timeboxes.

There may be multiple changes needed in an iteration. To simplify the work each 'micro' change can be managed in its own timeframe (as long as this does not exceed the time allowed for whole of the making progress activity). Some agile methods call this timeframe a sprint or a timebox, which is a concentrated period of time in which as much progress as possible is made.

These timeboxes or sprints are fixed in duration so that making progress can complete on time and the deploy/dismantle activities in realizing benefits can begin when agreed. This is very important because of the work involved in deployment, which affects many stakeholders.

The number of timeboxes is a product of the following factors: the number of people involved in the change, and the amount of work that can be grouped together as a concentrated piece of effort.

In some cases one individual can work on one specific change or a group of specialists may come together to resolve a number of changes. This division of labour will have been decided by those involved in the plan activity of the getting started process.

If there have been multiple timeboxes or sprints to create the change, it may be necessary to have a concluding timebox (shown in Figure 3.18

Figure 3.18 How timeboxes fit together

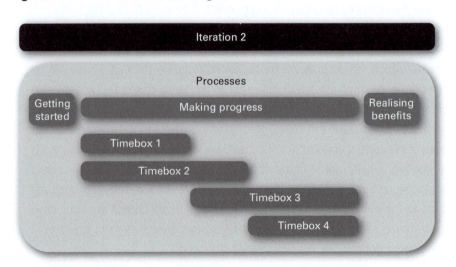

as Timebox 4) that brings together all of the individual changes and reviews them to see if they work together in an integrated way. Whilst each change will have been reviewed to ensure it meets its own acceptance criteria, a set of acceptance criteria for the integrated changes may also have been created, which will be reviewed at this point. It is important to understand that the individual changes do not contradict each other prior to moving into deployment where the live business environment will be impacted.

Making progress

Change

Changes are created by making alterations to existing processes, systems and roles or designing new processes, defining new responsibilities and implementing new systems.

To ensure the iteration meets its deadline this design work will be carried out in strict priority order, starting with those changes that are essential to realize the expected benefit. These must have changes are those that give the iteration its reason for being and if they were not made there would be no point in making any other changes.

Once they have been completed, important changes which would be painful to leave out will be designed, followed by those that are wanted or desirable but could be left out if time is short.

Test

Before the changes are implemented they will need to be agreed by others (review group) to ensure they meet their acceptance criteria. This might include a walk through of the proposed changes, a demonstration of new documents, databases, or a presentation of the newly configured end-to-end process.

At the end of the change work the prioritized requirements list will need to be updated to record what the team managed to include in the iteration and what had to be left out. This will then be reviewed and re-prioritized at the start of the next iteration.

The review activity is an opportunity to widen the number of people involved in the change. Being asked to evaluate the outputs enables individuals to have their first practice with the new ways of working which will help them become familiar with the approach and encourage them to become part of the change team.

Reviews can be used to evaluate individual elements of the change produced by a single timebox as well as testing how all of the changes fit together.

The acceptance criteria for this integration testing are likely to concentrate more on the usability of the process, eg:

- total duration;
- level of complexity, eg number of steps in the process, number of items of data required;
- resource usage, including the number of people required to carry out the work and the level of skill or experience they will require.

The acceptance criteria for individual elements of the change are likely to test the accuracy of the process and the accuracy and completeness of the outputs it produces.

Realizing benefits

For some changes there is a time lag between adopting the change, the realization of benefits. For example, improvements to levels of customer service and customer satisfaction will over time produce an increase in revenue and number of contracts retained or won. However, benefits of streamlined processes can be measured immediately, including metrics on the number of steps in a process, time taken to complete each step, number of pieces of work produced per hour etc.

The business case will define what benefits are expected as a result of the change and how these are to be proven. These measures should already have been applied to the business when they were used to generate data about the current state. In this activity measures are taken to prove that the new ways of working have produced improvements at least in some of the measures. This is because there may have been disbenefits or negative impacts created by the change which are unavoidable but deemed acceptable because they are outweighed by all of the positive effects of the change.

An important acceptance criterion for any of the 'specialist' iterations is that whatever change is produced contains elements that address the change from all perspectives:

- changes to processes;
- changes to systems including software, hardware, communication protocols and databases;
- changes to reporting lines and job descriptions;
- changes to measures of success, eg key performance indicators;
- changes to attitudes and behaviours;
- changes to relationships and levels of authority of those involved.

Deploy

Deploying the changes gives a further opportunity to generate support for the change by giving those that need to work in a new way a chance to practice through training and running the new processes alongside the old ones until an acceptable level of capability has been achieved.

The activities will have been agreed at the start of the iteration and should include sufficient support so that those using the new ways of working for the first time feel confident because they know they can turn to others for guidance and productivity will not be hampered by delays when individuals encounter situations that have not been covered in the training.

For these reasons, deployment should include the creation of temporary support structures to assist individuals with the implementation, including specially trained colleagues who are deemed to be 'super users' and who 'walk the floor' during deployment to provide on the spot help and advice; and dedicated helpdesk resources to resolve issues and assess if each problem is a result of special circumstances, or is more common and should be included in future training.

Dismantle

As well as introducing these changes, each iteration should include activities that dismantle what used to exist, and congratulate those responsible for the progress that has been made.

Dismantling is the removal of access to old ways of working. This might include physical removal of materials no longer required, or removal of access rights to systems and information or the dissolution of forums, user groups and schedules of meetings. Included in this are updates to operating procedures or quality manuals to include the new processes and remove information about things that used to happen. This dismantling generates motivation for further changes by ensuring the work environment does not become confusing or cluttered with a mixture of old and new ways of working. It also ensures that the environment is as simple to operate as possible which helps to reduce confusion over who does what, duplication of effort and time wasted.

Celebrate

Celebrating involves congratulating people on the effort they have made, proving the success of the change by measuring improvements that have been generated by the change.

Points to consider

What type of celebratory activities are relevant for your change, given the culture of your organization?

How will you know when Iteration 2 has been a success?

A good test of when change has been embedded is when it is no longer referred to as a change, but is 'just the way we do things around here'. Another indication is when people no longer talk about how they used to do things, which indicates they are no longer mourning the old ways of working and the power and competence that they felt that they had then.

These points apply equally to subsequent iterations of the change, recognizing that incremental delivery can lead to several iterations as the details of the change evolves.

This roadmap is meant to be adapted to meet the needs of your change situation and the culture of your organization. It has concentrated on the process of change, and will only be successful if it is used in conjunction with the relationship building skills described later in this book, along with the creation of an environment that supports the implementation of change.

Business need

04

Introduction

The purpose of any change initiative is to deliver what the organization needs, when it needs it. Change is disruptive; it creates fear and uncertainty and absorbs a lot of resources. It should not be undertaken unless it answers a specific business need.

In this chapter we will explore what business need means, and look at ways in which it can be defined and the many interpretations that are associated with it. We will identify how this information is used in each of the processes and activities described in the roadmap. The information gathering required to define the business need is not a one-off activity but is repeated throughout the life of the change. In the first instance, the information gained is theoretical, in that the change is still an idea being discussed. As we move through the life of the change, the information will be based on reaction to what has been changed so far and perceptions of how much more change is needed (Figure 4.1).

We will address the most difficult aspect of business need, which is that in order to understand the need and identify those changes that will deliver the most benefits, you must first understand the business. This understanding comes from your own understanding of what your organization does and information about the market in which it operates.

Knowledge of the business identifies who should be involved in scoping and defining what needs to change, and how information that is generated affects those involved. Once we have information about the change we need to know how to use it.

What this chapter does not do is repeat great swathes of information on benefits management or stakeholder engagement. These topics are covered in great detail in a number of excellent books. I have not assumed that you

Figure 4.1 Business need throughout the change lifecycle

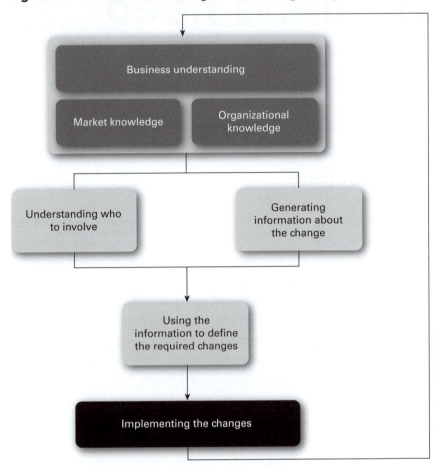

are a business analyst whose full time role is to translate business need into specifications and acceptance criteria. As with the rest of this book I have assumed that you are someone whose has been asked to lead a change initiative, as a result of your specialist knowledge or your position in your organization. This chapter explains the sort of information that you will need to use to prioritize this work to make sure that you are able to deliver changes that have a positive effect, delivering them incrementally, iteration by iteration, in such a way that the early iterations generate benefits that can help to fund the later iterations of the change.

What is business need?

The business need is the purpose of the change. It explains why the change is necessary. The term 'business need' is difficult to define because it means different things to different people. For example:

- the strategic goals or objectives of the organization;
- the problem that must be fixed or the opportunity that must be exploited;
- the level of performance that must be achieved;
- the creation of a specific desired outcome that has the support of staff or customers;
- anything that the business wants, when it wants it.

Figure 4.2 Integrating the elements of business need

Requirements
'features and functions'

Benefits
'measurable improvements'

Acceptance Criteria
'what does good look like?'

I believe that business need is a mixture of:

- the improvements expected (benefits);
- the level of quality that the change must meet (acceptance criteria);
- the features and functions that the change is expected to have (requirements).

It's important to clarify what each of these elements is and how you can use them to plan your change activities (Figure 4.2).

Benefits

There are lots of formal definitions for the term 'benefit', but to keep things simple we will view a benefit as an improvement that is quantifiable and measurable. So we need to review our change for all of the possible improvements that it creates. For example:

- Which activities and processes will be easier to carry out as a result of the change?
- Which activities and processes will require fewer resources as a result of the change?
- Which activities and processes will require less re-keying of data as a result of the change?
- Which reports will be automated instead of being manually collated as a result of the change?

For every improvement you have to quantify its size and scale, and identify ways in which it can be measured, so that when you have made your changes, you can prove that your change is beneficial. It doesn't matter what measures you decide to take to prove that the change has been positive, as long as you are able to define an objective statement that can be answered unequivocally, with a yes or no:

- yes, this benefit has been achieved, and here are the measures of what this factor was before the change and what it is today which proves that the improvement in the situation is real;

- no, this benefit has not been achieved, shown by these measures of the current situation versus the measures taken before the change was implemented which proves that there has been no improvement.

This is far more effective than subjective statements, which are personal views, feelings or perceptions. If the improvement is left without measures, asking those impacted if it has been achieved generates different answers from different people depending on their view of the situation. Change is an emotive subject and their perspective will be driven by their experience of the change, and whether they believe they have benefited or have been disadvantaged by it.

For example, if your change has been designed to create a streamlined process then the expected outcome of the change will be a reduction in the number of activities needed to complete a process, less effort needed to carry out the process and/or fewer documents created as a result of the process. To quantify the scale of the improvement you will need to know:

- how many activities there are in the process today;
- how many artefacts are needed as inputs to each of the activities;
- how long the process takes to complete from start to finish;
- how many people are involved in the process today.

Once you have this information you can estimate what these measures will be once you have made the change, and take measurements of each of these items after you have implemented the change to prove that the benefit has been achieved.

You will also need to decide exactly what to measure for each of these factors and how this information can be collected. Some information might be automatically generated as part of the process, eg start and end times, but there may be some manual work involved in counting each of the individual activities that everyone does by observing who does what.

To minimize the work involved in translating desired improvements into measurable benefits it's advisable to use existing metrics and performance measures, otherwise you could be in danger of creating a considerable amount of work to measure all aspects of the current situation before making any changes.

Fewer steps in the process is an example of a tangible benefit (ie a benefit that is real or actual). You should recognize that your change will deliver intangible benefits (ie those that do not have a physical presence). These include improvements to how people feel about their job, customer satisfaction levels and how easy or intuitive it is to perform certain tasks. In order for these intangibles to become benefits you have to identify how you will prove that the situation has improved and how you can measure their achievement.

Although intangible benefits are an indication of how people feel about a situation, their feelings can be measured before and after the change. For example, staff and customer surveys can be used or you could count the number of complaints or compliments received. Ease of use can be measured via error rates or the time taken to complete a process.

You should also understand what negative consequence might arise as a result of the changes. These negative consequence are called disbenefits, and it is important to understand what they are, how sizeable they are and who will be affected by them. After all, you should not be making any changes where the expected benefits for one group of stakeholders are outweighed by the disbenefits experienced by other stakeholders.

When deriving the benefits it is very important to identify the disbenefits – these must not be ignored because they are an excellent way of showing that you care about the impact of the change and recognize that it is not a positive experience for everyone. Only when you know the disbenefits can you show empathy to those that are being disadvantaged and help them to identify ways to overcome the issues posed by the change.

Acceptance criteria

Acceptance criteria are a measure of the quality that the change must meet. Effectively they are a statement of what good looks like and help us to judge if the change has been carried out in the way that we wanted. They are sometimes called performance criteria, critical success factors or non-functional requirements.

They help us to manage the risks associated by ensuring that the change doesn't affect the operating ability of the organization. Acceptance criteria can be regarded as a set of minimum operating standards and are likely to include targets for acceptable levels of:

- customer service;

- financial performance;

- data security and integrity;

- customer and employee safety.

To check the acceptability of the change you need to make sure that each acceptance criteria is written as a statement that can be answered with a yes or a no. There is no point having an acceptance criteria that cannot be assessed. For example, if you are assessing our newly streamlined process you might ask if it meets the following acceptance criteria:

- Does the process send a receipt to the customer or function providing the inputs?

- Does the process include a review of the accuracy of data after it has been input to the system?

Requirements

Requirements are an expression of individual creativity. They are an idea that someone has had for solving a problem or exploiting a solution, that if implemented will lead to improvements and the creation of benefits. They are often expressed as a shopping list of features, functions, purchases and new developments that will be needed and can range from big ticket items to very micro changes. For example, one person might request an upgrade to a system whilst someone else might request the removal of one field of data on an order form. The validity of each of these requests will need to be verified by:

- grouping the requirements into types or categories to get a sense of the nature of changes being requested;

- assessing each of these categories to try and identify duplicate items or items that are likely to conflict with each other;

- reviewing the requests to see if any of them are inputs to any of the others or if a requirement is dependent on other requirements.

Requirements need to be translated into specific changes that must be made. These changes must be reviewed against the acceptance criteria to make sure that they meet the quality standards. This can be accomplished through discussion to generate ideas and analysis, including the use of process maps, swimlanes and breakdown structures (explained later in this chapter).

Once they have been captured, the requirements will need to be prioritized according to their contribution to achieving the benefits, to ensure that if the change is terminated early the requirements delivering the greatest value have been included.

Points to consider

Who are the best sources of benefits for your change? Try and get a mixture of people to discuss the advantages of the change from different perspectives, including how it will impact how others view your organization and how it will feel to work in your organization after the change has taken place.

Where are the likely sources of acceptance criteria for your organization? Do you work in a highly regulated business where there are clear standards of performance, accuracy and service? Do you work in a creative industry where there are fewer external standards?

What categories of requirements are appropriate for your change? Consider grouping requirements by function or process or by level of quality, eg accuracy, security, speed etc.

Assigning information to type

Understanding the definitions for benefits, acceptance criteria and requirements helps us to make sense of the input we receive from others. People are messy, they do not talk in paragraphs where each statement that they make is clearly labelled as a benefit or a requirement. Instead their conversations contain a stream of ideas about the different features they want, descriptions of the improvements they would like to see, complaints about the current situation and rules that have to be followed to ensure their work is correct.

Case example

A professional services firm wanted to re-position itself in order to appeal to smaller companies and charities that had the perception that the firm charged premium prices and so was unaffordable. In announcing the desired transformation the CEO talked about the need to re-position their brand to increase sales across all services. He also described some of the changes that would be introduced including a move to Microsoft Office 365 and an expectation that all staff could access their work from office, home or client sites. This is a classic example of mixing up the benefits expected from the change (increase in sales) with a specific requirement (new IT system) and acceptance criteria (work accessible anywhere).

Translate this stream of information into an understanding of what you have to improve (benefits) and what you have to do to achieve those improvements (requirements and acceptance criteria). In the above example, you would need to assess what other factors the CEO is expecting to see as part of transformation. He has indicated that the benefit of increased sales will be achieved through a broadening of the customer base and a change to the IT platform. However, there will be many more requirements associated with an increase in sales and these will need to be identified along with relevant acceptance criteria.

Bringing the elements of business need together

The way in which benefits, acceptance criteria and requirements are applied will affect what the change will achieve.

There are two approaches:

- Requirements (also called solutions) led change focuses on the delivery of the new ways of working, irrespective of their capability to create measurable improvements. What is included in the change is driven by requests from those impacted by the change.

Figure 4.3 Requirements led change

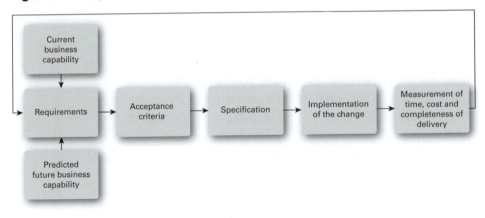

- Benefits led change focuses on the realization of the benefits and recognizes that there is no point undertaking the change unless it leads to measurable improvements. Only new ways of working capable of generating benefits will be included in the change.

Requirements led change

Requirements led change (Figure 4.3) is very common because it is the easier option. Those impacted by the change are asked what they want to see included. These requirements are drawn together into a specification which is implemented and the change is regarded as successful if this implementation is on time, on budget and delivers all (or nearly all) of what was originally requested.

This is a popular approach because it satisfies our need to be seen to be making progress. It values action over thought, with less upfront assessment of the importance or likely effect of each aspect of the change. Instead there is an underlying culture of 'just do it' that fits well with the time pressures that many of us work under and the assumption that being busy equates to being effective.

Requirements led changes are based on the assumption that because it was demanded by someone impacted by the change, the implementation of a requirement will automatically lead to improvements. The problem is that without defining how the benefit will be achieved it will not be known in advance if the requirement:

- will be capable of realizing the benefit;
- is the only approach capable of realizing the benefit;
- is the most effective use of resource to realize the benefit.

Case example

The marketing team of a large office supplies manufacturer had attended a digital marketing exhibition where they had attended several presentations on the importance of growing the database of potential customers. They had visited the exhibition stand of a well-known IT supplier and returned to their company fired up with enthusiasm for creating a new marketing database. The IT supplier had convinced them of the need for a new database management tool, and the team had been especially excited about the automated reports on customer segmentation that it could produce.

The team met with the marketing director as soon as they returned from the exhibition, and with her permission they arranged a meeting with the IT development manager where they presented their requirement for a new marketing database and explained that their director had already approved the funding for the change. In their minds, the job was done, ie they had identified their requirement, had been given approval by management and it was just a case of IT implementing the solution.

However, the IT development manager pointed out a number of concerns: the software recommended by the IT supplier was very expensive and the software would not integrate easily with the existing systems so a lot of new interfaces would be needed, leading to a long implementation time.

The marketing team campaigned hard to get what they wanted and accused the IT development manager of standing in the way of progress. However, they had jumped straight into a requirements led change. The IT development manager knew that what they really needed was instant access to website activity data so they could react more quickly to customer activity and generate more sales. If the marketing team had started with this benefit instead of their database requirement then IT could have built a simple interface between their existing systems and saved a lot of time and money, and would have provided the marketing team with the information they needed to react more quickly to customer activity. This would have created the benefit of generating more sales.

The requirements led approach creates the following issues:

- failure to fully investigate alternative scenarios, because the solution has already been decided;
- inappropriate influence by those in power to push forward their requirements;
- lack of willingness to accept the complexities in implementing the requirement, viewing those who raise these concerns as 'resisting change';
- failure to incorporate the views of all those impacted by the change, strengthening the belief that the requirement is the best solution because there have been no opportunities for others to challenge this view;
- lack of understanding of the benefits and disbenefits associated with the requirement, leading to non-existent or poorly defined business cases justifying the requirement.

Benefits led change

Benefits led change is the most effective approach because it creates a clear link between the improvements needed by the business and what is included in the change. It fits with the post recession era, which has increased the focus on achieving value for money. Benefits led change is more sustainable than requirements led change because benefits are stable, ie they unlikely to be subject to change because they are core to the continued existence of the organization. Requirements, however, can be very short term, based on the latest innovations in technology or business theories.

The advantages of the benefits led approach are:

- The use of resources is optimized. This is because:
  - all change activities are focused on creating value;
  - elements of the change are prioritized using the value of their contribution to realizing benefits.
- Creates 'feel good' content when communicating the change.
- Clear and simply defined explanations as to why the change is important.
- Provides an evidence based rationale for the change.

- The benefits or improvements set a boundary within which individuals from all levels of the organization can make changes to their ways of working, confident that they understand the bigger picture and what has to be achieved by their changes.

Benefits led change can involve a paradigm shift in attitude and approach to managing change. It necessitates that successful change is defined as the delivery of improvements and not the delivery of features and functions, even if they are delivered on time, on budget and to the required level of quality.

Case example

Benefits led change (Figure 4.4) means a change to our behaviours. It's vital that change managers move away from asking people what they think needs to change (which generates a long list of requirements based on personal preference) to asking questions about what needs to work better, what needs to be easier to do and what needs to impress the customers. Senior managers in several IT departments interviewed for this book explained that they no longer accept project requests from users unless there has been a session involving IT and the users that explores what the users are trying to achieve (ie problems they are trying to solve or opportunities they want to exploit) and the performance improvements they expect to see (ie what benefits they must deliver). Once everyone involved in the change has this common understanding they can begin to identify the requirements that will create the required benefits. The interviewees explained that these changes in behaviour have taken months to implement, and have required a lot of persuasion of users to give up their time to work collaboratively with IT, instead of seeing IT as a function that is commissioned to do whatever the users require. However, users are now starting to appreciate the approach, recognizing IT as partners who want to help solve problems and deliver them the best solution.

There is a logical flow to the benefits led approach which consistently and rigorously assesses the contribution of each aspect of the change:

- Benefits are driven by an understanding of current business capability that needs to be improved and the need to develop capability that meets future opportunities.

Figure 4.4 Benefits led change

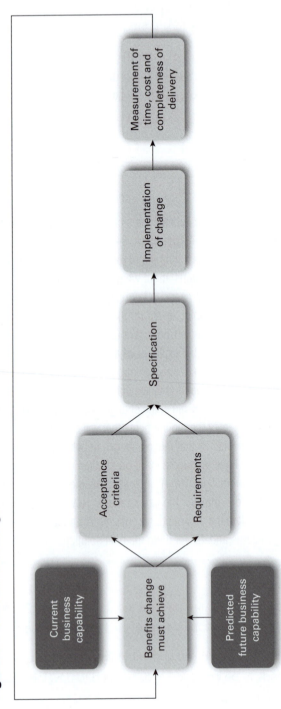

- Once the benefits are known they can be analysed for their acceptance criteria. These criteria act as constraints on the innovations that can be included in the new ways of working so it is important that they are relevant to the benefits and are not included 'because we have always met this quality standard'.

- Similarly, the requirements are only included if they result in an improvement to the current situation or are capable of positively exploiting a new situation.

- The need to meet a specific quality standard creates the need for a specific feature or function to be included in the change, eg the need to meet information security standards led to the inclusion of functionality that blocks access to payment data as soon as transactions are completed.

- The existence of a particular requirement identifies quality standards that must be applied to that feature or function, eg the inclusion of a payment facility on the website means our processes must meet financial regulatory standards.

The benefits led approach provides a strong foundation for managing change in an agile way because the benefits can be used to assess the priority of every requirement (Figure 4.5). The contribution of each of the requirements to the achievement of the benefits will define the importance of the requirement, which determines the priority of the requirement categorized as a must have, should have or could have.

Validity of the change

Combining the benefits, acceptance criteria and requirements creates the overall understanding of the change which leads to a vision and/or blueprint. This description of the change creates the sense that the organization is moving towards an exciting new future and is an important part of establishing the validity of the change. This validity is a personal assessment of the 'rightness' of the change by those impacted by it and determines how much support an individual is prepared to give to make the change a reality. This assessment of 'rightness' is based upon an interpretation of:

Figure 4.5 Benefits drive the prioritization of requirements

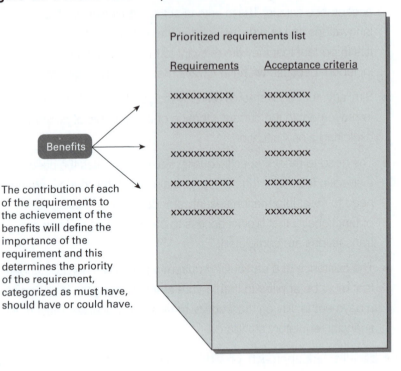

- the level of usefulness that the change is perceived to have;
- whether the change offers a logical, sensible and proportional response to the situation;
- the capacity for the change to achieve what it is supposed to achieve.

The validity of the change can only be assessed when those impacted can fully understand the change and set this into a context that makes sense for them. The validity of the change is an important factor in determining how much support there is for making the change and how willingly people will participate in its creation.

A lot of change practitioners interviewed for this book felt that their organizations made the implementation of change difficult by failing to communicate the information needed for individuals to assess its validity. An important piece of information needed to generate validity is an understanding of the background to the change. Understanding how senior managers came to the decision that the change is beneficial for the organization, critical to meeting customer need or important in maintaining or growing market share helps those impacted to decide for themselves that the change is necessary.

If those affected by the change are given a description of what will change without this background information about the business need, they may misinterpret their role in the change. The description of the change can be interpreted as an instruction to be followed and not a choice to be considered. Chapter 6: Environment explains the importance of choice in creating the motivation to change, and understanding the choices that those authorizing the change face when selecting the change can help to create a willingness to participate.

Whilst we could argue that employees have to follow the instructions issued, as change professionals we know that this unwillingness slows the pace of change because we have to cajole, encourage and persuade individuals to become involved, because they have limited personal motivation to participate, and closes access to extra ideas about the change, because individuals are insufficiently engaged, so they do not use their creativity to enhance the quality of change activities or ensure that nothing has been missed.

Points to consider

Review some changes that you have been involved in and decide if they were benefits or requirements led.

Aligning business need to the roadmap

The information about the business need is used throughout the lifecycle of the change. As you are managing your change in an agile way, allowing the details of the change to evolve in response to internal and external demand, there is a need to continually re-define the business need. Therefore, benefits, acceptance criteria and requirements are identified as part of preparing for the change in Iteration 1, and are used to decide how the change will be managed (Figure 4.6).

In Iteration 2 – and every subsequent iteration – the benefits, acceptance criteria and requirements are used to identify and create the specific changes that lead to new ways of working (Figure 4.7). They are revisited at the start of each iteration, at which stage additional information is generated to ensure that effort is focused on those requirements making the greatest contribution to benefits and any new requirements generated as a result of the most recent implementation of the change have been captured.

Figure 4.6 Role of business need in Iteration 1

Iteration 1		
Getting started	Making progress	Realizing benefits
Discover: Benefits are reviewed to understand the scale of the change, which will drive the level of formality required to manage the change. Plan: This level of formality will drive who to involve in planning how the change is managed.	Change – the initial requirements will drive the deliverables listed in the change description, which will be scheduled and resourced in the change management plan. The benefits will form part of the business case. The scale of the change will impact on the governance structure outlined in the change management strategy.	Deployment of the roadmap does not generate any of the benefits defined as part of the business need for the change, as these are realized as a result of Iteration 2 and onwards.

Figure 4.7 Role of business need in Iteration 2

Iteration 2		
Getting started	Making progress	Realizing benefits
Discover: Create or update the prioritized requirements list. Plan: Allocate the work in the prioritized requirements list across one or more timeboxes depending on resource availability and inter-dependencies of the work.	Change – create the changes needed to meet the requirements. Test – review the changes to make sure they meet the acceptance criteria.	Celebrate – the improvements generated by the change are measured to provide evidence that benefits have been realized.

How frequently are you reviewing what your change has to deliver?

How are you keeping your stakeholders informed of changes to the expected benefits, the requirements that the change will address or the acceptance criteria that it must meet?

Developing your business understanding

Your ability to lead change is directly affected by your level of understanding of the business that you are changing. Insufficient understanding creates the following situations:

- inability to identify the relevant questions to ask those impacted by the change so that a detailed understanding of what is involved can be achieved;
- failure to analyse trends and innovations outside of your organization to generate ideas about what is possible;
- difficulty in contributing to decisions on the prioritization of the benefits and the requirements needed to achieve them.

You need to develop business understanding about the market in which your organization operates and the capability of your organization.

I am not suggesting that you have to be an industry guru before you can effectively lead a change initiative, however it is important that you can set the potential change in the widest possible context so that every aspect has been considered, leading to the selection of the best possible course of action.

Market context

Understanding how other organizations work can trigger ideas about what to change in your organization. Whilst some of this knowledge might be competitively sensitive there will be a lot of information available about how your industry works.

As a consultant I work for lots of organizations and I have to be aware of the important issues in their industries. My technique is to start with a quick overview and then research any important points. My overview comes from:

- the company website – it is surprising how many staff have no idea what information about their strategic objectives, company history, vision and plans are on the internet;

- links from the company website to major customers, suppliers and regulatory bodies;

- white papers or testimonials that highlight key issues and achievements;

- any relevant industry bodies or professional associations which have regular webinars or seminars – even though I don't attend myself I make a note of the topics covered and look for any trends or common themes.

I do the same with any conference of exhibition websites relevant to the industry, reviewing the presentations from previous events and the course programmes for future events.

If the company is publicly quoted then I will search for analysts' reports and media commentary, especially relating to changes at board level which provide a good summary of the intentions of those new to the company and their past experience in other companies.

The factors to consider include:

- market demands and social trends;

- competitive pressures from existing competitors and those new to the market via start up companies or the extension of services by other organizations;

- development of products or services that have the capability to supersede what you currently produce;

- political and regulatory environment;

- available technology;

- industry best practice and standard measures of success.

Organizational context

Understanding how work is undertaken within your organization involves your knowledge of the specific practices that operate as a result of the culture and values of your organization and the practices that have built up over the years to address the specific needs of your customers and staff. Although you work for the organization, try and take a more objective view and consider the following points as part of your preparation for change:

- the values and behaviours that the organization is most proud of and which forms the public perception of the organization;
- productivity and skills of staff;
- internal political support for the proposed changes;
- likely customer reactions to the proposed changes;
- level of satisfaction with current range and delivery of products and services.

Case example

One of the interviewees for this book works for a specialist sports holiday company that is committed to excellent change management. The company is constantly changing their range of holidays so that they have new adventures to offer to their customers. The senior management team believe that this ability to constantly evolve what they are doing to meet customer need is their biggest competitive advantage, and their belief has been cascaded down to everyone who works for the organization.

Jane, the interviewee, is responsible for creating new adventures and she described their process to me:

The first step of our holiday design process is to pool our knowledge of what is happening internally and externally to get a feel for what we think might sell the best. We host a half-day workshop where representatives from IT, Finance, Purchasing and HR give us an up-to-date view of what is happening in the company including leavers and joiners, partnerships with suppliers and changes in contract terms, profitability, amount available for investment in product development, and projects close to completion or already planned or underway. Our external assessment comes from representatives from Sales, Marketing and Business Development who give us a review of what has been selling well or badly, customer feedback and the views of the local representatives who are running our holidays. From all of this information we create a range of ideas about enhancements to existing holidays and the creation of new adventures.

We then test our knowledge by inviting suppliers and customers to a panel discussion that is hosted by our sales director.

There is a 50/50 balance between staff and customers/suppliers and each member of staff is paired up with someone from outside the company. Obviously members of the sales and marketing teams attend but so do the sports specialists who source new activities to include in our programmes. It works really well and many of those attending the forum are the first to book on the new holidays.

It took some persuading to get senior managers to agree to these regular events because they were concerned about competitively sensitive information being shared amongst the suppliers, or customers thinking badly of us for 'doing our research in public'.

These concerns disappeared after the first session when senior managers realized how enthusiastic everyone was about the chance to contribute their ideas, and there is a much deeper knowledge in the organization now about what is involved in creating a holiday and marketing and selling it once it has been created which has increased the quality of the ideas that we come up with.

Business understanding questionnaire

There are lots of tools to help you perform a comprehensive analysis of your market and your organization, its strengths and weaknesses (SWOT analysis) and the market in which it operates (PESTLE analysis, McKinsey's 7S, Porter's 5 Forces etc).

However, it is unlikely that you want or need to bring this level of formality to the development of your knowledge. After all, we are working in an agile change environment that recognizes that change is constantly evolving. During the time taken for a detailed analysis things may have changed anyway.

For a more pragmatic view, use the questionnaire below as a guide to the type of information that will be most helpful when preparing for change. Keep your answers short and instinctive; as they are your viewpoint, they are not necessarily factual. However, they are your perception and you will use them to form your own opinion of the value of the changes so you must be aware of them:

- What does your organization do?
- Why does it do it?
  - because it is an established market leader in this area of business;
  - because it has a long and proud tradition in this area of business;
  - because this area of business is profitable and in high demand by customers;
  - because the founders have interest or knowledge of this area of business.
- How is the organization structured?
  - by product or service;
  - by location or country;
  - by department or function.
- Who are your competitors?
  - established firms against whom you have been competing for some time;
  - new entrants to the market who are smaller and react quickly to customer demand.
- How stable is the political/regulatory environment?
- Is your area of business subject to media scrutiny?
- Is there a lot of innovation in your marketplace?
  - What are the three latest innovations that affect your area of business?
  - Over what time period were these innovations launched?
- Who are your customers?
  - Is the number of customers that you serve increasing or decreasing?
  - Do customers have high levels of repeat business?
  - Are customers actively engaged in providing feedback on their experience with your organization?

- Why do your customers buy from you?
  - because your firm offers a unique product or service;
  - because your firm offers value for money;
  - because your firm offers quality of service.
- What are the biggest concerns for those running the company?
  - competition;
  - rising costs;
  - falling sales;
  - inability to pass on cost rises to customers;
  - regulatory changes;
  - instability in the supply chain.
- What would your organization like to be better at?
  - faster to market;
  - greater range of products or services;
  - greater efficiency;
  - increased profit margin;
  - more customers;
  - fewer complaints from customers;
  - operating in more locations.
- How are closely do these points align to the strategic objectives?
- Where does your area of expertise fit in?
  - What problems does your work solve?
  - What opportunities does your work offer to customers and those running the company?

Your level of understanding will be a product of your experiences. These will include the amount of time you have been working in your current role, current organization and industry. If you have had a stable career path with a long history at the same organization it is an idea to consciously build a network of external contacts through suppliers, professional associations, conferences and exhibitions. Colleagues who have recently joined from other organizations will have a useful perspective and be able to compare their previous experiences with what they have found in your organization.

Case example

If anyone joins my team from outside the company I ask them to give a short talk a couple of weeks after they have joined to tell us about the impression they have formed of the company – good and bad – and how it compares to where they worked previously. If anyone goes on a training course or attends a conference they are asked to prepare a 15-minute slideshow of the key things that they have learnt. I hope that this sends the message that I am very interested in what is happening 'in the outside world' and that it is important to keep expanding our knowledge.

Accessing a wider perspective comes from looking outside of your current area of responsibility:

- if you currently supervise the work of others, consider doing the work yourself for a day to get a more detailed understanding of the challenge involved;

- if you are the one producing the work checked by others, ask if you can shadow one of the supervisors to get an insight into what they look for when reviewing the work and the factors they have to consider;

- identify those relationships that provide input to your work or for whom you provide outputs and ask if you can shadow them so that you understand the origins of your work or how it forms the basis of other activities and processes.

All of this information helps you form an understanding of business need so that you can evaluate the importance of each of the elements of the change, and when necessary use this information to prioritize the work.

Points to consider

- Identify your level of business understanding by using the business understanding questionnaire.

- Within your team who has the strongest business understanding and what would you like to learn from them?

- What activities would help you to develop your business understanding?

Understanding who to involve

Using your understanding of the business environment helps you to identify who needs to be consulted about the change. We need to ask all those likely to be impacted by the change:

- what they expect the change to achieve (benefits);
- what elements they expect to be included in the change (requirements);
- what quality standards these new or amended elements must meet (acceptance criteria).

I know that 'stakeholders' is the accepted term for those affected (or who think they are affected) by the change but I prefer to use the word 'community' because a community is united by common interests.

Community map

All of those involved in your change can be represented on a community map which shows who they are and what their relationship to the change is.

The suppliers mentioned in Figure 4.8 are either internal suppliers (ie colleagues that we receive information or other inputs from that we need in

Figure 4.8 Community map

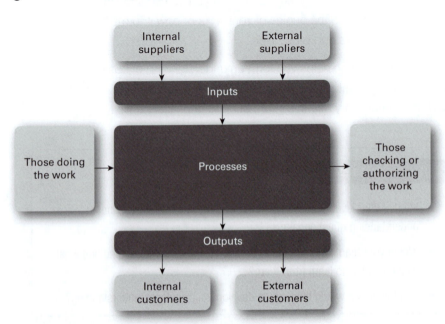

order to carry out our work) or external suppliers that we formally contract with to supply us with information, systems etc to be able to do our jobs. Their interests will include:

- Are there proposed changes relating to who they contact when they are ready to make a delivery?
- Are there proposed changes relating to how they deliver their products and services:
  - method of delivery;
  - timings of delivery.
- Are there proposed changes to the contract or service level agreement that they have with your organization?

The customers are either internal customers (ie other colleagues who use the work that is being changed to carry out their work) or external customers who will purchase the results of the work being changed. They are interested to know:

- if there are any proposed changes to how they are notified when the work is ready for them to use;
- if there are any proposed changes to when the completed work becomes available for their use;
- if there are any proposed changes to how the work will be packaged or made available to them.

From the user perspective, identify those doing the work and those that are checking or authorizing their work. Aspects of the change important for both of these groups include:

- Changes to how they do their work:
  - techniques and the skills required;
  - equipment and materials needed for the work.
- Changes to who they work with or who they work for.
- Changes to expected rates of productivity or acceptable error rates.
- Changes to the location of their work or the times at which they are expected to work.

This community map will need to be refreshed throughout your change initiative as the evolving solution will affect the relevance and importance of the stakeholders, with some fading into the background and others being added.

As well as regularly refreshing your community map, it is important to ask yourself if it is in balance:

- Are there similar proportions of existing and new connections – if there are too few new connections then you are probably viewing the change from too much of an internal focus, and you will need to consider how others who you may not currently be connected to are likely to be affected by the change.

- Is there representation across all roles or management levels within your organization? If you have only identified roles and responsibilities representing a narrow band of seniority, consider widening this out to include people at levels above and below those you have already captured.

- Is there representation across a wide range of functions and departments? In our interconnected world it is not possible to limit the impact of the change to only one area of the business, so look for other areas of the business that are impacted by the change. For example, consider those supplying information and resources to the function directly impacted by change, as well as those that supply them with inputs. Consider who the immediate recipients for your outputs are and who their recipients are.

- Are there similar proportions of people inside and outside your organization? In a small number of cases your change may be strongly internally focused so those impacted will be drawn only from inside your organization, but the majority of organization-wide change initiatives affect everyone in the ecosystem or environment in which your organization operates.

Points to consider

Review the roadmap and identify points when you are going to revisit your community map and update it.

Understanding others' perspective

It is important to try to understand the change from the perspective of those being impacted by it. By developing an understanding of how they are affected by the change you will gain an appreciation for the urgency and importance that this group ascribes to elements of the change, which must be considered when prioritizing the work. This prioritization affects what work is included in each of the iterations as well as deciding what work will be treated as must haves in an individual iteration.

Personas

A simple technique for considering the views of others is to write a 'persona' or 'characterization' that describes how the stakeholder is affected by the change. These personas are relatively quick to create and help to identify individual stakeholders but also the community of stakeholders engaged in the change (see Chapter 5: Relationship building).

Personas can be created for specific individuals or more generically to represent a group who are impacted in a similar way. As a minimum consider personas for each of the roles shown on the community map, as each of these groups will have a different relationship with the change. Keep the personas short and make sure they cover the same information for each stakeholder group otherwise it will not be possible to compare like with like. Suggested contents include:

- Name:
  - Create a name for each persona, which might be a category name or a real name to 'humanize' the analysis of the change.
- Position:
  - Name of their organization, job title and their level of seniority and/or reporting line.
- Power:
  - Level of authority or influence that they have in connection with the change. For example, do they have the authority to demand certain features or functions? Are they responsible for any part of the budget for the change? Will they be a signatory to any contracts with suppliers?

- People within your organization that they are connected with who are also affected by the change.
- Characteristics pertaining to the change:
  - Information on previous purchasing or supplying behaviour.
  - Daily, weekly, monthly or other types of regular tasks.
- Perceptions of the change:
  - Reasons why they are likely to support the change.
  - Issues or problems they are most likely to raise about the change.
  - Key outcomes that they would like to see the change achieve.
  - Why these would be of benefit to them.

Whilst the information contained in the persona will be based on your knowledge and assumptions, try to make it as accurate as possible by meeting with as many of those involved in the change as you can. If you cannot get access to customers directly then interview those in customer facing roles within your organization including sales/call centre staff, customer services teams, marketing and business development roles. Similarly, interview those who work most closely with the suppliers, including procurement.

Creating personal commitment to change

It is important to define the benefits from the perspective of the organization, but it's also necessary to encourage individuals to define benefits in a way that makes sense for them and answers their most important question ('what's in it for me?'). We need people to be committed to making the change, and this can be achieved by getting them to break down the organizational benefits into statements about improvements that they are going to take responsibility for. These statements then become their objectives and in turn they can get the buy-in of their team members by sharing them and asking their team members how they are going to be delivered.

There has to be a balance between the organizational need (people understanding why the organization needs to make the change) and what's in it for them. People will not participate in change that is good for the organization if it makes their life worse. There needs to be some 'win' for the individual so it is very important to listen at the beginning for ideas about what would make the change work for them.

A new automated appointments system was introduced to a group of delivery drivers, the purpose of which was to structure their routes and prioritize their calls. The system gave the organization much greater efficiency because it increased the number of calls that each driver could make in a day. However, the drivers lost their autonomy over deciding the order in which they could make their calls. In the early stages of understanding the change, the drivers had identified ways in which the change would impact their way of working and then suggested things that would make it go well. As the drivers were concerned about the increased number of calls they had to make each day, they suggested the installation of GPS in their vans to enable them to find specific addresses quicker and more easily. In fact, it was found that a number of drivers were already using their own GPS systems in their vans to help make their jobs easier.

Initially this suggestion was agreed which was an important 'win' for the drivers – however it was later decided that the cost of implementation was too expensive for the first wave of change. From the drivers' perspective, the change has led to more calls per day, without any improvements that make it possible for them to fit in more calls. Failing to include their suggestion about GPS has created the impression of win/lose – the company gets what it wants but the drivers don't get what they want.

Unsurprisingly, installation of the new tracking system led to almost daily complaints from the drivers. They expressed their dissatisfaction about being ignored by complaining about the lack of logic for the routes they were given, as they went back and forth across their areas.

The change manager believes that these teething problems would have been accepted, and the change adjusted to much more smoothly, if the drivers had been given GPS systems when the changes were introduced.

People form an opinion of change based on a wide range of factors. Some of the points they consider are:

- organizational benefits;
- likely achievability;
- personal benefits;
- past experience of change;

- attractiveness of the future;

- unattractiveness of the present.

An understanding of the strength of feeling on any of these factors will give you an idea of what to address with each individual. A quick way to assess strength of feeling is to ask people the following questions listed in Table 4.1.

Table 4.1 Motivation for change questionnaire

	Strongly agree	Agree	Disagree
Organizational benefits			
I believe that the changes are what our customers want us to be doing			
I believe the changes will increase our competitiveness			
I believe the changes will improve our reputation in the marketplace			
I believe that these changes are best practice in our industry			
I believe that these changes take advantage of new technology and/or innovations in our industry			
Personal benefits			
I feel my work will be more closely aligned to what the organization is trying to achieve			
These changes will give me greater opportunities to use my core skills and talents			
These changes give me an opportunity to learn new skills			
These changes will bring me into contact with a wider network of experts			
These changes will give me a chance to reduce my working hours			

Table 4.1 continued

	Strongly agree	Agree	Disagree
Likely achievability			
I feel the tasks involved in making the change happen are achievable			
I have a clear understanding of who will be involved and what they will be doing			
I feel confident that I can complete the tasks that have been assigned to me			
I feel the time allocated for the change is reasonable			
I believe the current levels of performance can be maintained during the transition to the new ways of working			
Past experience of change			
I have been involved in a number of successful change initiatives			
I have learnt new skills from my previous involvement in change			
As a result of my previous involvement in change I have increased my seniority and/or level of responsibility			
I have built new and productive relationships as a result of my previous involvement in change			
My enjoyment of my job increased as a result of the changes I have previously been involved in			

Table 4.1 continued

	Strongly agree	Agree	Disagree
Attractiveness of the future			
I believe that my input has been included in devising the new ways of working			
These changes create a more intuitive process			
These changes will reduce the amount of errors and rework associated with my work			
These changes will improve the timely delivery of my work			
These changes will make it easier to track the progress of my work			
Unattractiveness of the present			
Current workflow is badly organized with lots of delays			
There are currently a high number of customer complaints about the area that I work in			
I do not have the opportunity to use all of my skills in the current environment			
I do not feel that we are applying best practice or industry standards to how we currently work			
Our products and services are not as popular as they once were			

Case example

The senior management team of a packaging company that supplies storage boxes to removals firms decided to change its product range, creating a new range of cardboard boxes for sale to storage companies, who would then sell them to their customers.

This change affected the sales team, who needed to start building relationships with storage companies as well as those involved in design and production. The production manager leading the change expected everyone to be very positive as the organization had not been doing so well recently. However, as he didn't know much about the sales function, he began with a survey to assess the views of all those he was expecting to involve in the creation of the new product range.

He realized he had a lot of work to do to get people on board with the change when the survey results contained so many comments about their satisfaction with the current product range. Several managers commented on the success of their teams in hitting current sales targets and others made the point that change was unnecessary because customers were still buying from them.

This highlighted a worrying naivety at all levels of staff. There was no realization that the level of repeat business had fallen, that existing customers were placing lower value orders and that sales volumes had been maintained but customers were buying lower margin products, so revenue was stable but profitability was falling.

The production manager had to amend his change plan, adding in workshops to identify the benefits of the new product range, and asking members of the senior management team to participate so that they could help explain the current business environment and why they thought creating sales with storage firms was so important.

Without the survey, the production manager would have started the change with activities on design and developing the product range, which would have failed to generate the support needed from the sales function to adapt to the change by creating new relationships and new sales demonstrations suitable for storage companies.

For a quick summary of the results from all those participating, represent the number of 'strongly agree' answers from the Motivation for change question-naire on Figure 4.9 to see where staff are in support of the change (or use the chart to capture the number of 'disagrees').

Figure 4.9 Measuring support for the change

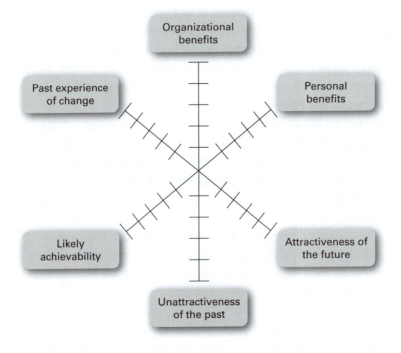

In Figure 4.10 the individual has had excellent past experiences of change and this may have influenced their positive feelings about its achievability. They are not particularly attracted to this change, so greater communication of its benefits would be useful.

In Figure 4.11 the individual has a strong view that the change will be positive for them and the organization as a whole. However, they have not had good experiences of change in the past and so more information about how the change will be managed would be appropriate in this case.

Figure 4.10 Example of poor support for the benefits of change

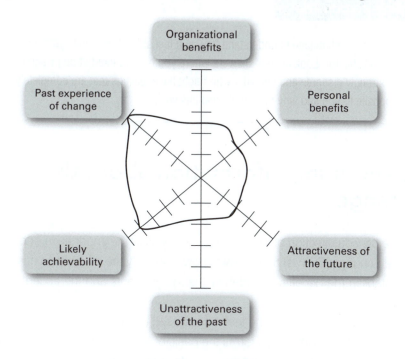

Figure 4.11 Example of poor past experience of change

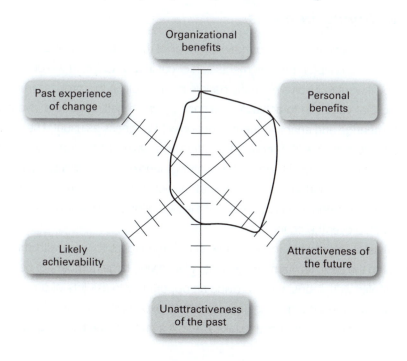

Points to consider

Use the questionnaire to understand how you feel about the change you are responsible for. Look at your answers where you have marked strongly agree or strongly disagree and consider who might have feelings that are completely opposite to you and why they might feel this way.

Generating information about the change

In the previous section of this chapter we identified the importance of benefits led change. This section explains how to identify the information needed to establish the benefits and identify the requirements and the acceptance criteria.

Figure 4.12 shows how the techniques used to create the benefits create a benefits description which forms the basis of the identification and prioritization of the requirements and the acceptance criteria.

Identifying benefits

Identifying benefits uses information from all of the steps we have described so far in this chapter. Improvements can occur in any aspect of the business so you'll want to involve as many people as possible in this process, recognizing that you have to achieve a balance between getting people involved in the change and enabling them to get on with business as usual. The more people you involve, the more information you have to assimilate, which is also time consuming. However, by involving people you are giving them one of their first opportunities to participate which builds a team atmosphere and enables people to take control of their situation and develop a sense of ownership over the change.

Whilst it is possible to ask a few senior managers to work with me on defining the benefits, I am an advocate of involving large numbers of people in benefits workshops which provide an opportunity to ask lots of questions about how the change originated, what is expected to be included and when changes are expected to take place. It's unclear whether the quality of

Figure 4.12 Business needs process

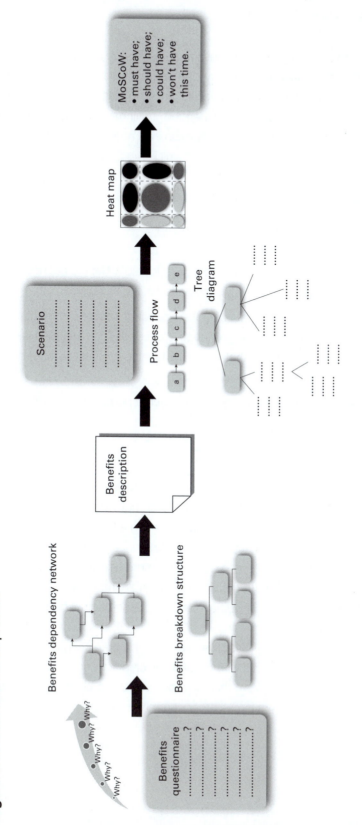

information is any better because more people are involved, however I suspect that it is because the diversity of those involved gives the widest possible perspective on the change. Even if there is no material difference in the quality of the benefits information generated, I still have the advantage of getting people on-board, whose participation I will need at every step.

A simple technique that works well for individuals and groups is to ask people what single improvement they would like to see as a result of the change. By asking for one idea:

- You are reassuring people that they don't have to do a full analysis of every aspect of their work.

- It makes those who have a clear idea of what the change should include consider why it is needed in the first place.

- It's possible to get a useful snapshot of people's immediate perceptions of where change is needed. Their one idea is usually the area of business that they think has the greatest number of problems or offers the best opportunities.

- One idea multiplied by the number of people we ask still generates a lot of information.

Five whys

The five whys technique was originally devised by Sakichi Toyoda who helped to create the lean and six sigma methods. It is a simple technique that starts with the change manager asking a business representative what they think is the most important improvement and also why it is an improvement, which allows them to generate a more detailed answer. The next step is to ask why this more detailed answer is an improvement and so on, over four or five cycles until we have expanded the original benefit into as much detail as possible.

Figure 4.13 is an illustrative example of a marketing director discussing changes to the website with the aim of including more links to social media.

As you can see from this example, whilst the discussion began with a simple improvement in customer communication, the ultimate benefit is an increase in sales.

Figure 4.13 Five whys example

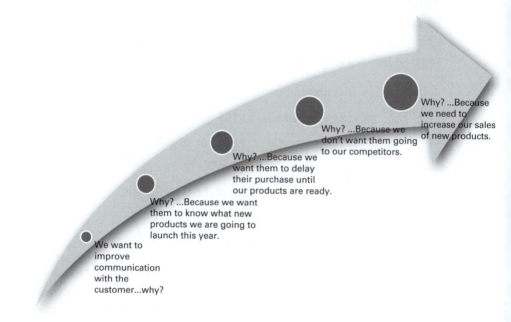

Why? ...Because we need to increase our sales of new products.

Why? ...Because we don't want them going to our competitors.

Why? ...Because we want them to delay their purchase until our products are ready.

Why? ...Because we want them to know what new products we are going to launch this year.

We want to improve communication with the customer...why?

Points to consider

Take one improvement that you believe your change will create and that you have an in-depth knowledge of and expand it using the five whys technique.

- How many whys are you able to identify?
- Have any of your answers surprised you?
- Have you identified more positive aspects of your change?

Benefits questionnaire

In some situations we can generate more information about the benefits if we provide people with a pre-defined benefits questionnaire that helps them to develop their thoughts. The questionnaire solicits information across all types of improvement, so begin by identifying the areas of the business that you would expect to see improve as a result of the change and then create questions that enable those taking part to consider if there will be improvements in this area and be able to describe the type of improvement they are expecting.

A sensible source for these categories is the strategic objectives of your organization. For example:

1 increase profitability;

2 generate cost reductions;

3 improve customer service or customer satisfaction levels;

4 improve the perception and reputation of the organization;

5 improve the competitive position of the organization;

6 improve staff engagement and retention levels;

7 adhere to a new legal or regulatory requirement.

These benefits or improvements may look very high level and outside of your remit. Obviously ultimate responsibility for the achievement of these strategic objectives rests with your board of directors, but it is helpful to understand how changes taking place many layers down in the organization, often altering specific processes and ways of working, can directly contribute to these bigger goals.

Increase profitability

1 Is there a desire to be able to charge more for existing products and services which would imply a link to improvements in competitive position and/or improvement in the perception or reputation of the organization?

2 Does the change involve launching new products or services with fewer competitors enabling the organization to charge a premium for them?

Generate cost reductions

1 Does the change streamline existing processes so that fewer staff are required to do the same amount of work?

2 Does the change reduce the number of inputs to existing processes so that the cost of supply is reduced?

Improve customer service or customer satisfaction levels

1 Will improvements to customer service lead to an increase in the number of repeat purchases, referrals by satisfied customers or retention of existing customers?

2 Does retention of the customer base increase the opportunities for cross-selling and increasing the overall spend per customer relationship?

Improve the perception and reputation of the organization

1 Will the change lead to higher levels of quality, establishing the organization as a premium brand?

2 Will the change improve customer service levels or competitive position generating good news stories about the organization in the press?

Improve the competitive position of the organization

1 Does the change enable greater innovation and lead to the launch of products and services not offered by the competition?

2 Does the streamlining or simplification of a process reduce the time to market so products and services can be launched ahead of competitors'?

Improve staff engagement and retention levels

1 Will the change increase the positive perception that staff have about working for the organization?

2 Is this improvement linked to a greater ability to offer good service so customers complain to staff less, or does it offer a greater feeling of wellbeing because the organization has an improved reputation or competitive position in the market?

Adhere to a new legal or regulatory requirement

1 Does the change enable the organization to comply with new legal requirements?

2　Does the change enable the organization to more easily prove that it complies with legal requirements, so is linked to cost reductions in liability insurance?

Don't forget that these questions should also identify any negative side effects of the change, ie disbenefits.

Points to consider

Review the benefits questionnaire and see if you can add any additional categories of benefits relevant to your organization and the type of change that you are making.

What questions can you ask about this additional category?

Benefits breakdown structure

A benefits breakdown structure provides a format for subdividing a specific improvement into all of its constituent parts.

For example, if the expected benefit of the change is to have fewer steps in the process, the benefit can be broken down into specific aspects of the work where the benefit might be felt, which in this case includes accuracy, resources and training (Figure 4.14).

Alternatively, the benefit can be broken down into types of benefit, the two most common types being cost reduction and revenue generation (Figure 4.15).

To create a breakdown structure each factor must be broken into at least two sub-factors. If a factor can only be broken into one sub-factor then this is not a breakdown, this is just a renaming of the original factor. It is this need to keep breaking each of the factors into more sub-factors that generates ever more detailed information about the benefit. Using the example above, we use the breakdown approach to further develop our understanding of the Training benefits (Figure 4.16).

It is this detailed understanding that will enable us to identify how each of the benefits is to be measured. In this example reports detailing how much has been spent on printing course materials and hiring training rooms can be compared with the situation after the process has been streamlined to see if there has been a fall in costs.

Figure 4.14 Benefits broken into types of work

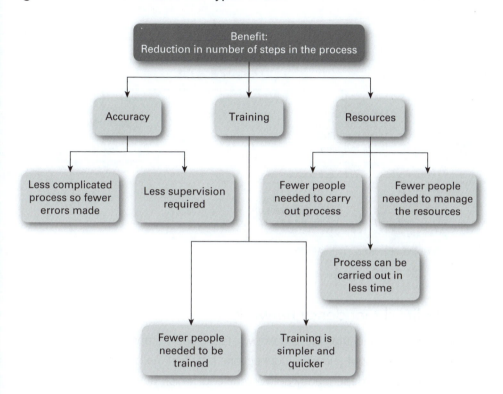

Figure 4.15 Benefits broken into types of benefit

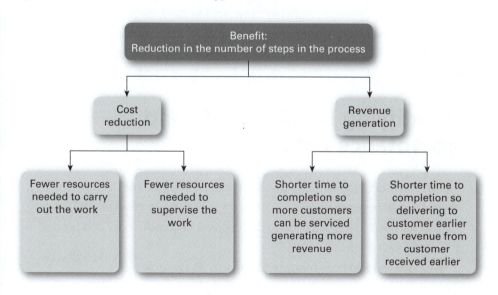

Figure 4.16 Benefits broken into sub-factors

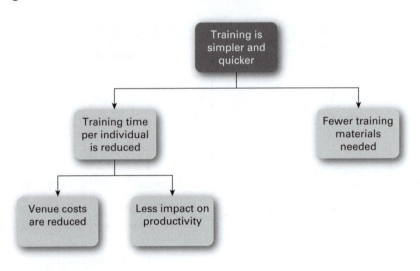

Benefits dependency network

Some people find that the breakdown technique hampers their thinking because it does not show the connections between the benefits. Consider using a benefits dependency network instead, which develops more information about the benefits by asking the question: 'what happens next?' This can include unintended consequences which might be positive or negative, ie disbenefits.

In Figure 4.17, the relationship between the benefits is clearly shown, which helps to identify those benefits that enable other benefits. So even if a benefit is quite small, its importance increases if it enables other benefits.

Identifying requirements and acceptance criteria

Information about the benefits is used to identify the features, functions and required level of quality that the change must deliver. To generate this information we need to use knowledge of the current situation to try and predict the new ways of working.

We need to identify as many requirements as possible:

Figure 4.17 Benefits dependency network

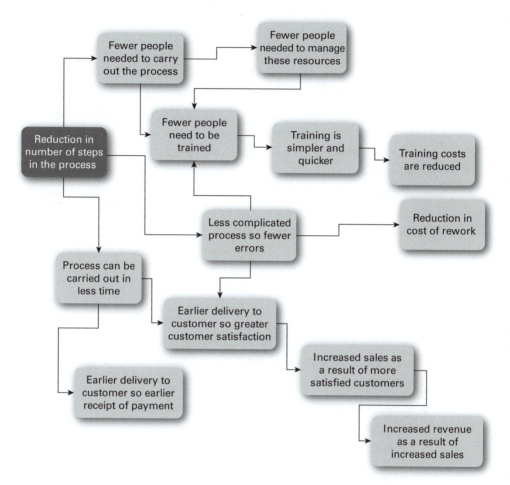

- The more ideas we capture, the more alternatives there are to choose from, increasing the chances that we are implementing relevant and value generating change.

- Requirements identified ahead of implementation can be scheduled and resourced, whereas failure to identify them upfront means unplanned work that leads to delays.

Once the requirements have been identified they can be reviewed to give an understanding of where the impact of the change will be felt. This is an important consideration when prioritizing the change activities as there must be a balance between creating new ways of working and continuing to deliver business as usual until all of the changes have been embedded and have become the new business as usual.

It is likely that we will expand the number of people participating in the change from those that were involved in identifying the benefits. Involving those impacted by the change in the requirements gathering exercise enables them to have a degree of freedom and autonomy over their work which is likely to motivate them to become involved and remain involved in the change. If an employee's role is restricted to implementing changes defined by others, then they are not being given the opportunity to work out how to make the change work for themselves, resulting in a loss of a sense of ownership or control. Instead these people find themselves working in a situation where all of the thinking, creativity and innovation has already been done by others and they are simply following instructions, which is not motivating.

To avoid this, we have to give everyone the same opportunities to identify how change will affect them:

- Those in more senior roles have not performed menial tasks for many years. Trying to predict the exact specifics of the change from a more senior position guarantees that a lot of the smaller changes will fail to be identified. Therefore, the planned change is almost guaranteed to fail.

- Those in more junior roles do not authorize or audit the work of others so will have fewer ideas about the quality standards and key performance indicators that the requirements must meet.

An obvious difference in perspective is driven by the view of the world that each of the business representatives has. In its simplest form, some of them will describe the requirements for the change as a vision of the future state, looking towards new opportunities and new capabilities that do not exist today. Others will describe the requirements in terms of solving problems that exist today, and moving away from the current situation via a number of improvements which they will describe.

There must be consultation across teams so that people can design the change in a way that meets their context. This overcomes the problem of people thinking 'we will not adopt this change because it has not been invented by this team'. It is a failed assumption that change designed and proven to be working in one area of the business can be easily transported to another area of the business.

Each area of the business has its own specific context based on the team members' past experience of change as well as their specific technical knowledge and experience, their skills and the team dynamic. It is not possible to achieve economies of scale in change by skipping over the investigation of the change (represented in our roadmap as the discover activity) because you assume the change will be the same in the other teams. They have to go through this period of investigation for themselves.

Whilst a lot of information is generated about what needs to change, it is not possible to predict every aspect of change. One small change has the capacity to trigger lots of other changes. A balance has to be struck between the amount of effort engaged in defining what has to change and the need to move swiftly to realize benefits.

Using an agile approach, the techniques outlined below which help gather detailed information will be repeated at every iteration which reduces the amount of planning at the start of the change. By skipping all of this detailed analysis at initial stages you are able to move quickly, reducing the risk of changing circumstances and needs. This agile approach encourages the solution to evolve, empowering those making the changes to respond to the effects of the change, increasing the relevance of what they are doing and improving the chances that benefits will be realized.

Process maps

For those driven by a need to improve the current situation, a technique that aligns with their approach is the mapping of the current end-to-end process, showing how the suppliers and customers interact, and defining the inputs and outputs used in or generated by each of the activities in the process. The improvements required can then be mapped to each of these elements, clarifying how the process will be different in the future. If the required improvement is a simplification or streamlining of the process then a new version of the end-to-end process should be created, as comparison with the existing process identifies what has been removed.

Improvements can be made to processes and systems that are used by a large number of staff or to a process that is only used by one individual, who has to change their specific way of working in order to remain aligned with how others are changing. To minimize confusion, get people together in a workshop to map the end-to-end process so that everyone is using the same information to generate ideas about what needs to change.

Figure 4.18 Process map

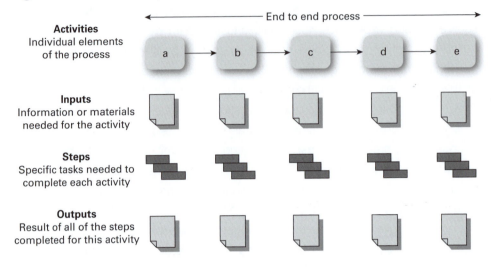

There are lots of different ways to create process maps and I have used a very simple approach shown in Figure 4.18. There are lots more examples to be found in books on business analysis.

Once the end-to-end process has been established, lead the discussion on the required changes by asking all those involved to select their preferred changes from a range of suggestions that you have already prepared. This ensures that the conversation remains focused on identifying improvements to the process, rather than degenerating into an unproductive discussion on how the process currently works. For example, suggest the eradication of certain inputs or outputs or suggest the removal of specific activities. Another way of leading the conversation is to ask the participants to make specific changes to the end-to-end process. These might include:

1 identify three pieces of new information that can be drawn together from other parts of the organization to create a deeper understanding of the customer or supplier relationship with the organization;

2 take three steps out of the process;

3 take out one document, report or form from the process.

Another simple approach is to take one idea from the latest customer survey or customer complaints or compliments file and see how it can be implemented. You can also develop the end-to-end process into swim lanes that show the different people involved, with each role represented by a separate lane (Figure 4.19). This can help to identify how often activities in the process

Figure 4.19 Swim lanes

Step 1:
Set out each of
the activities in
the process

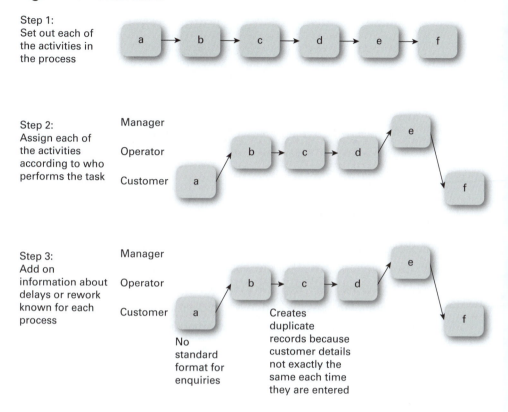

Step 2:
Assign each of
the activities
according to who
performs the task

Step 3:
Add on
information about
delays or rework
known for each
process

bounce back and forth between other people. This generates suggestions for change including co-locating groups to minimize this 'traffic' or enhancing the responsibilities of an individual so that they carry out more activities and there is less transfer of work to others.

Points to consider

Practice creating a process map by identifying all of the elements of an existing process that you know really well.

Use your information to quality assess other aspects of your change, eg are all those supplying inputs to your process or recipients of the outputs captured in your community map?

Have you written personas for them so that you can appreciate their perspective about the change?

Figure 4.20 Tree diagram level 1

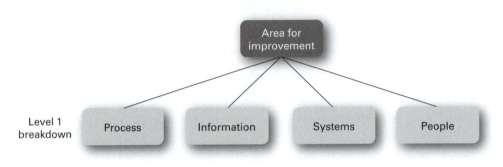

Tree diagrams

If those helping to define the change are good at articulating what is wrong with the current process, but are less able to identify how they think things should work in the future, document what they are telling you in a tree diagram. A tree diagram replaces the end-to-end processes with groupings based on the areas of the business likely to be improved by the change.

In this example, the areas of improvement are processes, information and data, systems and infrastructure, and people, including the number of people involved, their roles and the organization structure that binds them together.

Level 1 of your tree diagram should break the required area of improvement into the key factors that might need to be changed, eg processes, information and data, systems and infrastructure, and people, roles and responsibilities and skill levels (Figure 4.20).

Level 2 captures information about what is wrong with the current situation (Figure 4.21).

Level 3 captures ideas about what is causing the problem, which become things that your change initiative has to address (Figure 4.22).

Points to consider

Use the information you created for your process map to create a tree diagram.

What additional questions do you need to ask about your process to create the tree diagram?

Figure 4.21 Tree diagram level 2

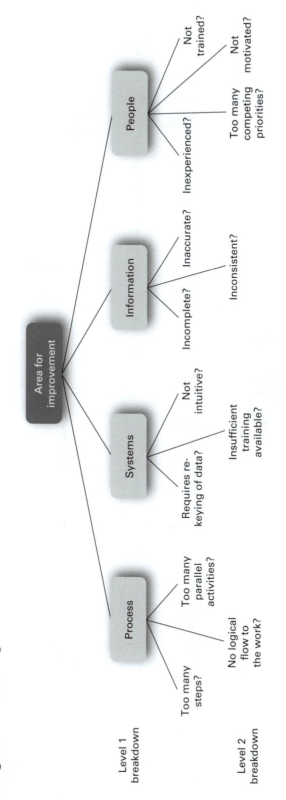

Level 1
breakdown

Level 2
breakdown

Area for
improvement

Process

Too many
steps?

No logical
flow to
the work?

Too many
parallel
activities?

Systems

Requires re-
keying of data?

Insufficient
training
available?

Not
intuitive?

Information

Incomplete?

Inaccurate?

Inconsistent?

People

Inexperienced?

Too many
competing
priorities?

Not
trained?

Not
motivated?

Figure 4.22 Tree diagram level 3

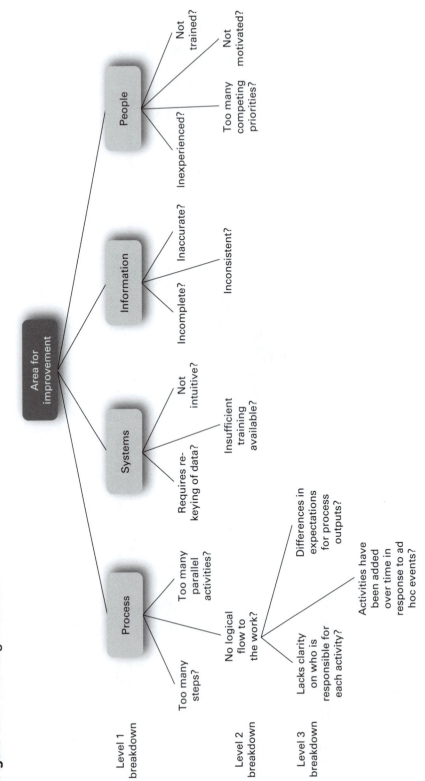

Scenarios

An alternative to mapping the processes is to identify the different situations that the new ways of working need to address and from these identify how the work will be undertaken. These descriptions of the situations are called scenarios and they are similar to personas (see pages 105–06) in that they tell a story, reflecting how people talk about their work.

Creating scenarios is a useful technique when those from whom we need to generate information are uncomfortable or unfamiliar with business analysis techniques such as process mapping.

Scenarios can be a useful technique when circumstances are so different that very little of what happens today will transfer to the new ways of working, so trying to map the changes on an end-to-end process would cause confusion, and those involved in creating the new ways of working have limited understanding of what happens today and would find it difficult to break the work into processes and activities.

A scenario provides a detailed description of a specific situation, explaining what caused it, what work is involved, who carries out the work and what they produce as a result of their work. They are created by those working in the area of the business that is going to be impacted by change.

This information can help us ensure we have identified all those that are likely to be impacted by the change, as the identification of different situations will help us to see who is involved in the situation and how they contribute to the work. We can then include them in the community map.

Most of our work addresses a number of different situations that can be divided into two types: normal situations – the work we expect to be doing as routine; and exceptional situations – the work we have to do to respond to previous failures or unusual or one-off requests.

To make sure you capture all of the different situations consider using a table to define what needs to be included (Figure 4.23).

Consider including the following information:

- each location where business is undertaken – office name, geographic location etc;
- type of customer based on regularity of purchase, size of purchase, purpose of purchase;
- the full range of products and/or services offered by the area of your organization that is being changed;

Figure 4.23 Tables of required scenarios

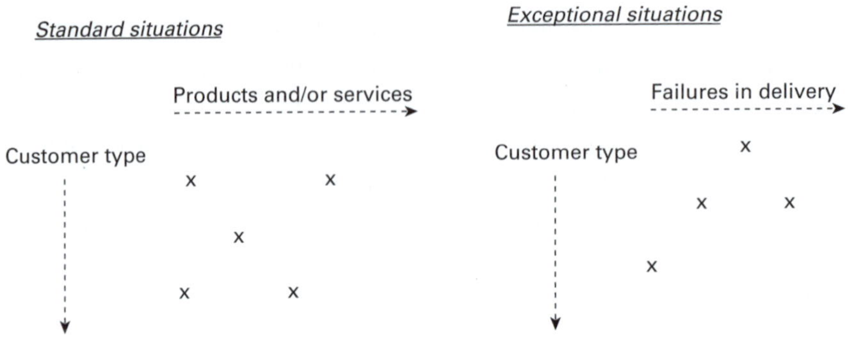

Standard situations   _Exceptional situations_

Products and/or services   Failures in delivery

Customer type   Customer type

- examples where exceptional situations can occur, usually driven by failures in the delivery of the original service including late delivery, delivery of incorrect product or service, poor customer service when delivering product or service.

Points to consider

How many different scenarios will it be useful to create for the change you are responsible for?

Defining the impact of the change

As soon as you have generated information about the requirements and acceptance criteria you need to identify the scale of the change and try to understand how disruptive it is likely to be. One of your responsibilities in leading change is to ensure that the level of change does not cause so much disruption that it negatively affects the normal business operations.

There are numerous examples of organizations that have become overwhelmed when they have failed to predict how much work is involved and how many resources will need to be dedicated to the change at the expense of their normal work. I know of one organization that struggled so badly to implement a new enterprise-wide management system that they neglected their existing customers. Their revenue reduced so much during the period of change due to poor service that the finance director has estimated that it will take them at least three years to return to the level of sales they had before the change initiative.

The scale of the impact will help you to understand how many people will need to be involved and how great the threat is to normal business. It is an important factor in deciding what aspects of the change to treat as high priority and what will only be included on a 'best efforts' basis.

Heat maps

A 'heat map' is a useful technique for showing the scale of the change felt by individuals or groups along with the number of changes they are involved with. A heat map is the term given to colour-coded charts that visually demonstrate the relative importance of the information. Commonly a heat map will use red (hot) to indicate significant impact and green (cool) to represent limited impact. To ensure all of your heat maps judge like for like you will have to agree a scale. For example, you might decide that if the change impacts less than 20 per cent of the work or the people involved then it has a limited impact but if it affects more than 70 per cent then this is regarded as significant.

Figure 4.24 Example of a heat map structure

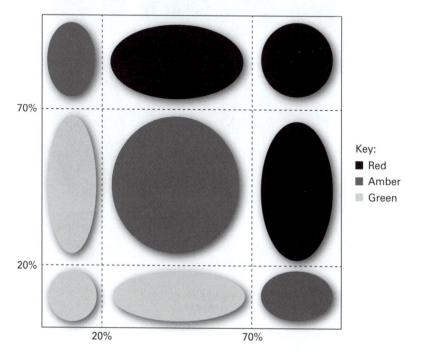

To evaluate the impact, consider the following factors:

- proportion of staff impacted;
- proportion of customers impacted;
- proportion of the workload that is affected;
- importance of the work that is affected.

The 'heat map' enables you to assess whether the sum total of the changes taking place is balanced across a variety of teams, processes, customer groups etc or if the impact is isolated to only a few staff or pieces of work (Figure 4.25). For example, an assessment of the impact of all of the teams in a department, reviewing the importance of the work impacted and the proportion of their work affected, might identify that only Team B is significantly impacted by the change, which reassures the head of department that as a whole they are unlikely to be overwhelmed by this change.

Figure 4.25 Heat map showing who is most affected

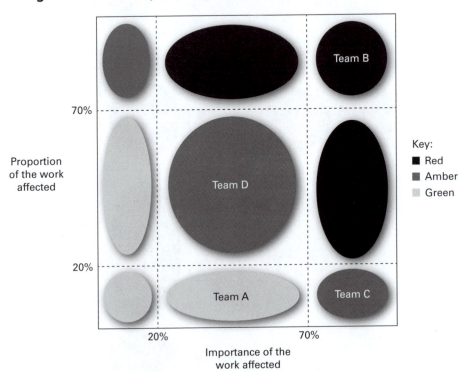

This initial assessment could be followed up by creating an organizational heat map that shows exactly who is most and least affected by the change. In Figure 4.26, we know that Team B is the most affected but there are a number of individuals in Team C and Team D who are significantly affected by the changes, but as their other team members are not impacted, the impact on the team is amber.

Similarly, a process heat map can be used to identify exactly where in a process the change will be felt. This is also helpful in quickly defining if the process is affected at the start or the end which might lead to changes being required in the inputs or changes to the availability or mechanism by which outputs are made available. For example, there are two activities that are significantly impacted in this end-to-end process, one of which involves the direct use of an input from another process, so we know that as a minimum those responsible for providing the input will need to be involved in our change (Figure 4.27).

Heat maps can also be used to indicate the total level of change being felt in a process or team, and not just the impact of one specific change. After all, as change is endemic in our organizations, there is a very strong possibility that other changes are taking place at the same time as ours, which may have a destabilizing effect on the business as a whole.

When we ask people to assess the size of the impact on their ways of working, we must remember that their answers are subjective. It is important to challenge this perception. To reduce these anomalies, define the factors that should be considered before assessing the impact.

These factors will be specific to the type of change you are making, but should include consideration of:

- changes in the complexity of the work and the associated skills required;
- changes in the quality of the working environment including privacy, noise, space;
- changes in the level of autonomy that individuals have to carry out their work;
- changes to conditions of employment including pay, hours and place of work.

Several change practitioners interviewed for this book raised the risk that these subjective assessments of impact often skewed the results towards a

Figure 4.26 Organizational heat map

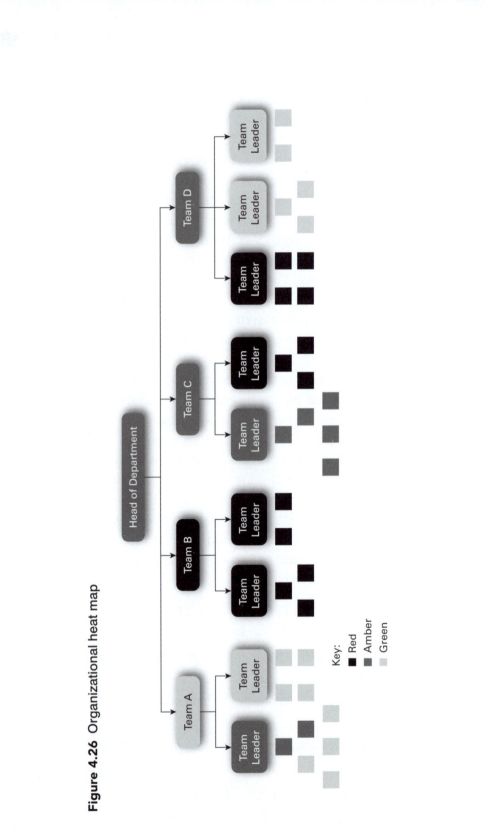

Figure 4.27 Process heat map

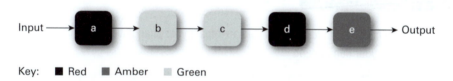

Key: ■ Red ■ Amber ▢ Green

much bigger impact than was actually the case. Several interviewees gave me examples of re-location projects where staff overestimated the negatives and underestimated the positives considerably.

It is not possible for us to validate all of the data that we are given about the change. However, we should sense check the results of the heat maps and be prepared to challenge the results if they seem out of line with our original impression of the change. This might involve observing people at work so that you can compare how they believe they are going to be impacted with what is actually happening in their role.

Case example

As part of the implementation of a new administration system, a team of administrators had assessed the impact on their work as very significant, even though the initial process mapping had identified very little change. I was assigned to sit with this team for a day to see how their work flowed and to identify the specific changes that would take place once the system was live. What I found was that there was a great deal of concern about preparing the weekly statistics because this module had not been discussed when the change had been presented to the team. They had assumed that there was no automatic reporting and that they would have to return to the manual collation of data – which they all hated. It was a simple issue to resolve, but had their original analysis not been challenged, it would have affected the roll-out schedule for the new system, as this team of administrators had been scheduled last so that their work would not be affected until everyone else was on the new system. This is not what the IT team wanted, but the heat map indicated this was the best course of action. Once the reporting issue was resolved, the heat map was re-drawn to show this team as green, ie limited impact, and they were re-scheduled to become the first to use the new system.

> **Points to consider**
>
> Use the heat map to identify how big an impact your change will have on the teams in your department.

Prioritization

It's vital that each requirement and its associated acceptance criteria are prioritized according to their ability to deliver the expected benefits of the change. First, work on the top priority requirements, and when this has been achieved, re-prioritize the remaining requirements and any new ideas that have come to light. Once this is complete, make further changes to incorporate the highest priority changes, and re-prioritize again throughout the life of your change.

In an agile environment, several versions of the solution will be deployed, with this deployment taking place at the end of each iteration. What will be deployed will be discussed and agreed in the discover step, and then the plan step will identify the activities and resources needed. See Chapter 3 for a fuller explanation of these activities.

Prioritized requirements list

In each iteration you will need to consider what work is most important and what can be left until later, which is carried out using the prioritized requirements list. All the requirements are captured on this list. Nothing is removed from it, but as the understanding of the change develops, more requirements will be added, and earlier requirements that are no longer seen as essential for creating the benefits will be given a lower priority.

The change initiative begins with the creation of the first version of the prioritized requirements list. This is used to scope the work of the second iteration (the first iteration does not involve the requirements for change, as it concentrates on creating the controls and governance used during the change initiative). At the start of the second iteration, a second version of the prioritized requirements list will be created to reflect knowledge about the change that was developed in Iteration 1, with further versions created at the start of each new iteration.

Figure 4.28 High level prioritized requirements list

Original prioritized requirements list

Prioritized requirements list:

Requirements	Priority
xxxxxxxxxxx	Must
xxxxxxxxxxx	Must
xxxxxxxxxxx	Should
xxxxxxxxxxx	Could

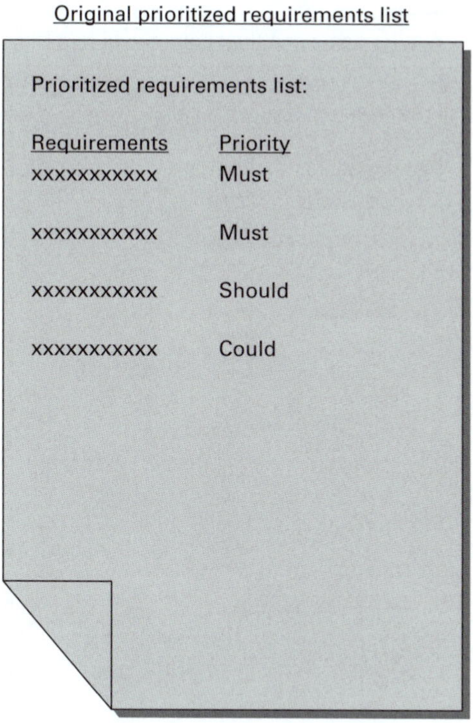

In Chapter 3 we discussed a well-respected prioritization technique called MoSCoW, which categorizes each of the requirements in one of four ways (must have; should have; could have; won't have this time):

Must have requirements are those that are essential to realize the expected benefit. These requirements cannot have a lower priority because there are no alternative ways of working that would generate the same benefit and if they were not included there would be no point in the change taking place.

If you are not sure if the requirement is a must have, try and imagine how it would feel if you were told that the requirement could not be met and cannot be included in the change (Figure 4.28). If at this point you realize that the change is pointless without the requirement then it is a must have. However, if you start to think of ways around the problem then it is probably a should have or a could have.

To ensure that the must have requirements are truly must have, break them down into smaller activities and identify from each of these which are must have and which are now should have or could have (Figure 4.29).

Figure 4.29 Detailed prioritized requirements list

Prioritized requirements list with
requirements and their component parts

Prioritized requirements list:

Requirements	Priority
XXXXXXXXXXX	Must
XXXX	Must
XXXX	Should
XXXX	Should
XXXXXXXXXXX	Must
XXXX	Must
XXXX	Should
XXXX	Could
XXXXXXXXXXX	Should
XXXX	Should
XXXX	Could
XXXXXXXXXXX	Could
XXXX	Could
XXXX	Could

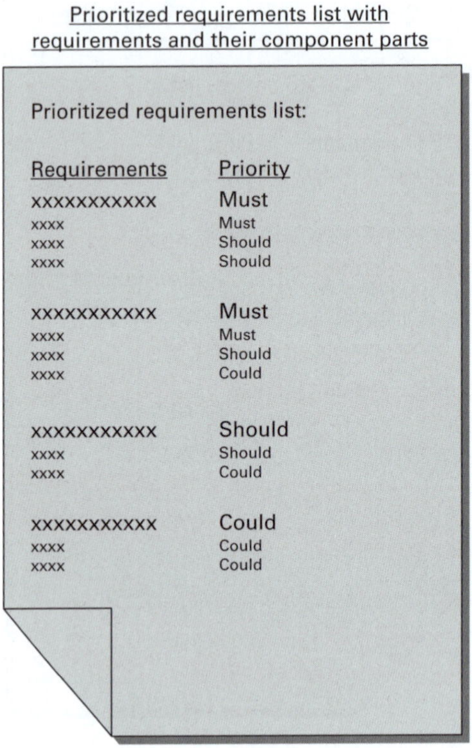

The second version of the prioritized requirements list shows how each requirement has been broken down into its component requirements. These can then be prioritized in their own right to understand if they are a must have or can be assigned a lower priority so that only the most essential aspects of each requirement are guaranteed to be included in the change.

Should have requirements are those that would be painful to leave out. They make an important contribution to the change but they are not essential like the must have requirements. There are likely to be potential workarounds if they were not included in the change but these alternatives are likely to be slower and/or more labour intensive and expensive.

Could have requirements are desirable but if they were not included, the majority of the benefits could still be realized. Workarounds exist that are capable of replacing them and these workarounds are not as negative as those associated with the should haves, because they impact fewer people, don't affect service levels as badly or are not as expensive to use.

Won't have this time is a useful way for capturing ideas that for reasons of cost, time, complexity or availability of resources are going to be left out. A requirement can only be put in this category if it has been assessed and there is agreement that it is not an essential contributor to the realization of the benefits of the change.

When the prioritized requirements list is reviewed during the discover step, new requirements will be reviewed and allocated to one of the categories. Earlier requirements that have not been implemented in the previous iteration will be re-prioritized. It is important that every idea is captured as it is not always clear when a requirement is first identified how important it is to the delivery of the benefits. Reviewing it in relation to all of the requirements establishes the importance of the requirement. Those requirements that are not viewed as capable of making a significant contribution to the benefits will be placed into the category of won't have this time. Once the change initiative has been completed, the won't have this time items, along with any should have and could have items that did not get included in the change, can be reviewed and may form the basis of a subsequent change initiative.

Techniques for deciding on the priority of requirements

Use these techniques to gather information that enables you and those impacted by change to define the importance of each element of the change.

Importance assessment – to help you decide how important the requirement or acceptance criteria is and therefore, which priority it is given, answer the following questions:

- Business value:
  - Can the benefit be achieved with any other workaround?
  - Does the requirement generate a sizeable benefit?
- External market factors:
  - Is it already offered by the competition?
  - Have others in the supply chain eg wholesalers or brokers requested it?
  - Has this functionality already been adopted by the market place as standard?

- Has this element of the change been specifically requested:

  - By an individual customer?

  - By a group of customers?

- Compliance:

  - Has it been demanded by regulators?

  - Is it a quality standard?

- Interdependence with other requirements:

  - Is it needed to enable something else to work?

  - Without the change will other things stop working?

  - Have promises already been made or expectations raised about the inclusion of this element of the change? If these promises are subsequently broken what are the consequences?

- How many other things depend on this element of the change?

Whilst the contribution to benefits is the key driver when deciding on the priority order of the requirements, it is also worth considering the practicality of the requirements. For example:

- availability of skilled resources to make the changes;

- number of changes affecting a specific system or process at the same time;

- ease of implementation;

- intuitive nature of the change;

- number of interdependencies.

I am not implying that harder changes should carry a lower priority, but it is sensible to create a balance in each iteration between complicated changes requiring specialist and limited resources and those changes that are easy to implement, easy to understand and have few – if any – effects on other areas of the business.

This prioritization technique will be applied multiple times during the life of the change:

- every time those making the changes engage with the business representatives to acquire more information about what is needed;

- every time a new iteration of the change begins because as must have requirements are delivered after every iteration, the remaining should have and could have requirements are reviewed and reprioritized.

By identifying the must have aspects of the change we are effectively creating the critical success factors for the change because we are stating that the change will only be a success if it is capable of achieving X, Y and Z.

Identifying the should have aspects of the change helps to identify where back-up plans may be required if the change cannot deliver all of the requirements. This is because should haves are something that the change team would like to deliver, but if they encounter problems old ways of working or alternative (often manual) ways of working can be used instead. These requirements are should have rather than could have because although there is an alternative, it will be painful for the organization to invoke its use. This is because the alternative is likely to be slower, or involve more people or deliver outputs in a format not seen as desirable by customers.

Could have requirements are useful but if they are not delivered the change is still capable of delivering the expected benefits or improvements, although the change would have been perceived as more desirable if the could have requirements are included.

Story telling Another technique for helping to understand the priority of the requirements is to create a story about the change. A story explains how the requirements are applied to create a new way of working, explaining how things are done in the new way, who is involved, where activities, inputs and outputs are dependent on each other and how the quality of the work is assessed and what happens if re-work is required. A story captures the totality of your understanding of the change helping to organize your thoughts into a logical explanation of what you think you have been asked to do, why it is important and who is involved.

The benefits of creating a story are:

- it is a way of organizing your thoughts into a logical flow that others can follow;

- it helps you identify any gaps in your understanding, because the story will not flow if you have missing pieces of information;

- it becomes familiar to you and therefore becomes normal to you, so the more you tell the story the more you lose your fear as the change is no longer new or unknown to you;

- it is easy to tell others, which provides you with opportunities to test out your own understanding and give others the opportunity to test their understanding and challenge your perspective.

There are lots of ways in which you can construct your story about the change, and the order of the information will be driven by your personal preferences, but to make sense to others, as a minimum it should contain:

- summary of the change – what is going to happen, when it is going to happen, where it will happen etc;

- reasons for the change – this is why it is happening, this is how it originated and these are the factors that led to the original idea for the change;

- benefits of the change – the results of the change and who will benefit and if relevant who will lose out as a result of the changes.

These are the key elements of the change – describe what will change based on your perspective. Your thoughts might primarily be about processes that will change, or the products and services, or the customers or marketing activities etc.

The first and last point that should be included in your change is the purpose of the story – this is the 'call to action', ie the action that you want others to take as a result of hearing your story. The 'call to action' might be a simple request to prepare for the change by tidying up any outstanding issues so that people will have time to become involved in the change, or it might be that you are telling them about the change as you have planned some training for them to take part in. Whatever it is, you need to be clear about the call to action before you create the rest of the content for your story, as what you say will need to persuade people to take the necessary action.

The story will be used consistently throughout the life of the change and it will evolve as specific elements of the change are defined in each iteration.

Conclusion

Understanding the business need is essential for ensuring that the change is relevant and will improve rather than worsen the current situation. It is a complex subject because it requires analysis to understand the need for the change from the perspective of your organization and market, and you will require highly developed interpersonal skills to enable you to build trust and empathy with those from whom you are seeking information about the business need.

This chapter has explained the technical skills and techniques for acquiring information about the business need and analysing it to form the scope and requirements of the change.

In Chapter 5 we look at ways of engaging with others to generate this information. We will also look at how to create a working environment that encourages people to define what they need from the change and identify what benefits it will generate for them.

Relationship building

05

Introduction

In an agile change, those impacted by change continually emerge as the solution evolves and the effects of the change become better understood.

Relationship building skills therefore are critical to the success of change; change managers need to be able to work cooperatively with individuals and groups who emerge as the change progresses and are not easily identified at the start. Understanding the community involved in the change is an important early step in our change activities but it is one that we need to regularly repeat. This continuous 'scanning' of our environment helps us find more people with whom we need to build relationships, ensuring that we are involving them in the change initiative as valuable team members, clarifying their role and giving them clear direction about what is needed. (See the section on 'Understanding who to involve' in Chapter 4.)

The purpose of many of our relationships is to persuade people to work differently. Change cannot be forced upon others; each person has to decide for themselves whether it is in their interests to do things differently. The role of the change manager is to positively influence people's view of the change, by demonstrating your own commitment to it and the advantages that others would gain from it.

Our ability to influence others is based on the strength of the relationship that we have with those we are asking to change. Do we appear to have integrity? Can we be trusted? Do we demonstrate the personal characteristics that make others want to follow us? In any situation in which you are asking others to work differently, you are establishing yourself as the change leader, irrespective of your job title or position of seniority. It is the personal characteristics of trust, integrity and empathy that are the foundations of your leadership ability, and which determine the breadth of influence that you have.

All of us have a particular 'sphere of influence' where we are naturally seen as the leader by a particular set of individuals. It's important to understand our natural sphere of influence and look to develop this to ensure it encompasses all those who you need to involve in the change.

Establishing relationships in which others are prepared to follow your lead involves building trust and demonstrating empathy with others. This is only possible if you understand yourself – how you prefer to work and how you want to work with others.

Relationships are a product of emotional intelligence, which is the ability to monitor our own and others' feelings and use this knowledge to define our thinking and actions. In this chapter we look at how to develop our emotional intelligence to be able to lead ourselves and the steps involved in building relationships with others.

Understand yourself before understanding others

Before we are able to build effective relationships with others we need to understand how we behave and what triggers our behaviour. We need a clear understanding of the effect that our behaviour has on others and a willingness to use this knowledge to actively decide how we should react to situations so that our attitude and behaviour helps us achieve our goals and does not sabotage our efforts.

Understanding ourselves is a product of personal awareness – knowing yourself, and personal leadership – controlling yourself.

It is this combination that leads to empathy with others, which is the foundation for building effective relationships.

Personal awareness

Personal awareness is the ability to know yourself, because if you understand how you react in different situations and what triggers your reactions then you can use personal leadership to proactively decide how to behave rather than simply react to a situation. This personal awareness has a significant impact on your ability to lead others through change as they will base their reactions on how you react.

Case example

Jane was a change manager working on a difficult set of changes which required the cooperation of many parties. She was responsible for building consensus and getting everyone to agree on what to do. She worked in a busy, open plan office alongside others working on different aspects of the change.

After every meeting Jane would walk back through the office either in a good mood or more often in a very bad mood depending on how the parties had behaved. She didn't realize (although her boss noticed) the impact her behaviour had on the rest of the team. Jane's boss became very concerned that when her meetings went badly motivation fell as people picked up on her despondency. He met with her soon after and explained the effect she was having on the team. She was very surprised as she had not realized that she was showing any emotion after her meetings or that she was having an effect on her colleagues.

After the meeting with her boss Jane was careful to compose herself before going back to her desk. She learned the value of taking time to decompress and calm down before returning to her colleagues so that she could portray a calmer and more balanced view of the situation to those around her.

Personal awareness is formed of two elements: self-assessment – understanding your strengths and limitations, knowing your preferred approach to your work, your likes and dislikes; and emotional assessment – understanding what triggers your emotions, appreciating how these affect others.

Self-assessment

As we have established, in order to form effective relationships it is imperative to be able to understand ourselves. In areas where we believe we have strengths and talents we are likely to come across as confident, capable and trustworthy. Where we have limited skills we may be more hesitant, lack understanding and have a greater need to rely on others for support and specialist expertise.

Self-assessment is formed of two elements: knowing your strengths and limitations; and understanding your preferences.

Knowing your strengths and limitations

As will be explained in Chapter 6, there is a strong link between what we are good at and what we prefer to do, but it is understanding these preferences that will help us to build the most effective relationships with others. At the most basic level, to achieve our objectives we need to build relationships with those who can fill the gaps between our core skills and preferences and what is needed to make the change a reality. We can only seek out those with complementary abilities if we really understand our own abilities. The opposite is also true in that knowing our strengths helps us understand what we have to offer others and how we can appear as someone worth building a relationship with.

There are lots of psychological profiling tools that can be used to help us find out what you are best at and what you most enjoy doing, but for the purposes of this book I am going to keep things simple and state that there are two things to remember:

1 you have things that you enjoy doing, find easy to do and you have certain ways that you like to approach your work;

2 to be as productive as possible you need to maximize what you enjoy doing and minimize the time you spend on those tasks you are not naturally skilled at and that you do not enjoy.

To help identify your strengths and limitations, use the list of change management activities in Appendix 5 to define what you want to do and ideally what you would ask others to do for you.

Understanding your preferences

We all have our own preferred way of working which are products of our personalities, previous experiences, likes and dislikes. For example:

- we have a preference for which tasks we do first and which we leave until later;

- we have a preference that guides what information we think is important and what we think we can ignore;
- we have a preference for whether we work alone and silently or in a group with lots of noise.

These preferences help us make sense of the world. There is so much information that we are subjected to every minute that our brain has devised its own way of looking at the world, and sub-consciously filters all of the incoming information to meet our needs, backing up what we already know and often discarding information that does not fit with our view of the world. There is some truth in the clichés 'we only see what we want to see' and 'we only hear what we want to hear'. That is why in any given situation two people can have radically different memories of what happened, because they have each filtered what happened against their own preferences.

As part of our personal assessment we need to be aware of these preferences so that we can recognize how we may have interpreted a situation and more importantly how others might have seen it differently. This appreciation helps us build relationships with others because we can understand that they are not expressing a different viewpoint because they are trying to oppose us, but instead recognize that their personal 'filters' will have given them a different perspective that is just as valid as ours.

For example, I know I have a strong preference for action over debate. My self-assessment tells me that in meetings, for example to plan the launch of a new service, my preference is to filter out any negative information about why aggressive deadlines cannot be met. My preference is to avoid discussions about the risks of moving too quickly because I interpret that as others coming up with reasons why the service cannot be launched, which I view very negatively. Knowing my reaction is driven by my preferences, I have to use my self-control and consciously remain listening when others are discussing risks.

Understanding our preferences helps us identify who we need to build relationships with. By knowing how we filter things we can ensure that the change team includes people that look at things from different perspectives. By working alongside those with different approaches, the widest possible range of change activities can be identified and undertaken.

This is a more challenging approach than forming the change team with those who share our preferences, because we often have a natural affinity with those who see the world from the same viewpoint as ourselves. As a result, we have to work harder to build common ground with those with different preferences, but it will widen our understanding of the change and increase the number of ideas and activities used to implement the change.

Case example

Liz works as a freelance change manager and has to build a change team each time she takes a new assignment. She uses a quick trick to make sure she doesn't surround herself with others just like her, which would narrow her range of abilities and make the work much harder. She knows herself so well by now that she has created a list of her preferred activities and what she thinks are their opposites before looking for those who like doing what she doesn't!

For example, Liz likes detailed plans, organizing her work with schedules, creating to do lists and knowing what she is supposed to be doing next week and next month. Liz's opposite meanwhile enjoys spontaneity and is more accepting of spur of the moment requests. While Liz uses her feelings to evaluate situations so that she can make quick decisions based on a skim through the available information, her opposite will wade through detailed information, happily cross-checking it and analysing it for its completeness and identifying any gaps.

Creating a balance of preferences and skills within the change team ensures there is capacity and willingness to tackle a wide range of change activities, and reduces the possibility that some tasks will not get done because no-one is interested in them or has the capability to address them.

Preferences guide our behaviour in two ways:

1 how we express our understanding of a situation;

2 how we generate our understanding of a situation.

Review the announcement of a recent change and identify what you believe to be the three most important pieces of information.

Re-read the announcement and identify three other pieces of information that you believe are unimportant.

How would your reaction to the change be different if you were told that your unimportant pieces of information were essential to the change, and your important information is merely of interest but not essential?

How we express our understanding of a situation Our preferences shape how we describe the change as well as the information that we share because we view it as important. At the same time we discard information that we do not view as relevant.

Some individuals impacted by change feel most comfortable assessing and describing the effects of the change in relation to what is happening today. This group of people will naturally describe the change in terms of:

- advantages and disadvantages in comparison with current working practices;

- how the change will solve problems and difficulties that exist today;

- how the change will offer new opportunities in addition to what happens today.

This is fine if those impacted by the change are responsible for enhancements to current working practices, but if the change is more radical, and abandons current systems, processes and measures of success then this group may find it difficult to conceptualize the change. This means that those impacted by the change continually refer back to the present, talking in terms of things that should be preserved from the current situation or things that should be avoided because they do not work well today.

If those impacted by change exhibit these preferences then their contribution might not include lots of innovation but they can provide useful quality criteria that the new situation must meet. They also provide a useful link back to the past and can help avoid making the same mistakes that have been made previously, so have a role to play in risk analysis.

Others impacted by the change may have a preference for avoiding any reference to what happens today and instead view the change from the new opportunities that it offers. They will describe the change in terms of how new it is, how innovative and how different it is from the past. They will set it in the context of how they see the future and how they anticipate others will react to it. These people are good at remaining focused on the goals and objectives of the change and are very good at imagining how things will work if they were given a blank piece of paper.

They are unlikely to contribute much in the way of risk analysis as they find it difficult to see potential problems or barriers to success. They may not be as comfortable if their implementation of the change is limited by constraints imposed by the current operating environment.

Regardless of whether those impacted by change make sense of the change in terms of the current or future situation, another factor that governs how they express the situation will be their preference for detailed information. Some people have a preference for looking at the bigger picture and viewing the change in broad terms. They are good at expressing the vision, objectives, purpose and benefits of the change but dislike identifying every activity needed to make the change a reality. If these people are given lots of detailed information, their preference will be to filter it to find the important ideas, sentiments and key tasks only.

Others can only become engaged with the change if they are given the opportunity to define the detailed tasks and activities, how they link together and how they might be affected by other initiatives. They have a talent for creating detailed research, analysis and plans.

Table 5.1, overleaf, shows how we may express our understanding of the situation.

How we generate our understanding of the situation Our preferences affect how we question, review and engage with the change so that we are able to form an opinion and acquire the information we will need to take part in the change.

Some of us who are responsible for leading change initiatives need to gather reference material about the change so that we have a conceptual understanding of what the change is and how it will affect how we work

Table 5.1 How we may express our understanding of the situation

Future	Detailed information	Will describe the new role in terms of what they will be expected to do each day, week and/or month. Will name their new colleagues and describe what they are responsible for and will describe the new activities that they will be involved in.
	High level summary	Will describe the new role in terms of new responsibilities, new people that they will be working with and new skills that they will be learning.
Present	Detailed information	Will describe the new role in terms of what is different to what they do today. Will specify what remains the same and information, infrastructure and skills that will still be required in the new world.
	High level summary	Will summarize the changes in their role, working environment and people they work with in comparison with the current situation.

before we engage with it. This preference leads us to seek out user guides for how things work, research papers that explain how certain decisions have been reached or detailed plans that explain the activities involved as well as what we can expect to happen and over what time period.

Another preference is to immediately engage with the change, acquire practical experience about it and form your own opinion of it based on your experiences. If you have this preference, you will most likely not wait to be given instructions or information but will be keen to 'have a go' and start trying out the change as soon as possible. For those with this preference, models, test suites and opportunities to pilot the change are important sources of information. See Iteration 2 of the roadmap in Chapter 3 for more information about modelling.

Alternatively, you may have a preference for understanding the change from the perspective of how others have experienced it. In this case you will want to be given lots of information upfront and will happily attend briefings and presentations or read information about the change, but will want an opportunity to consider how it will affect you before engaging with the change. Perhaps you will want to consider how others feel about the change before making your own mind up. If this is your preference, user groups and reference sites can be important sources of information.

In Table 5.2, overleaf, you can see how someone who is changing jobs will gather information about their new employer prior to starting their new job. The different preferences illustrate the differences in approach and the different types of information that will be gathered. As change leaders we need to ensure that the information we provide about our change meets the needs of all preferences, and is not created solely to meet our own preference.

Knowing how I build my understanding of new situations helps me recognize when I might appear impatient or disinterested in the way others behave. I have a very strong preference for gathering background information and ensuring I feel well informed before I take any action. I don't like to have a go until I understand the history, context and expectations of the situation. This makes me impatient with those that jump in and start work without taking time to do the research. The analytical part of my brain knows this is what they need to do to get comfortable with the situation but emotionally it makes me feel as if I am slipping behind and I worry about appearing unenthusiastic or disengaged. I am also irritated by those who feel the need to ask everyone else what they think before getting involved themselves as I don't think the experience of others is that relevant or helpful as every situation is different.

By recognizing my preferences I have been able to come up with ways of bringing these different approaches together. For example, I allocate a couple of days for people to absorb their ideas about the change, make sure there are plenty of opportunities for them to research it and review how others have experienced it or tried it out or seen it in action. I then convene a workshop to share all of these experiences and pool our collective knowledge.

Points to consider

Think of the last time you had to learn how to do something in a new way.
Did you gather background information first?
Did you ask others for their experiences of how they learnt this new skill?
Did you just give it a go and learn as you went?
Did you wait until you felt that the skill was important to your role before
  engaging?

Table 5.2 Differences in approach to gathering information about the new employer

Theoretically	Very keen to gather as much information about their new company as possible. They will be pleased to receive an information pack about the company from HR, and they will go through each page of the company website getting to know the background to the organization, its strategic objectives, details of who is on the board etc. They will search the internet for articles and analysis about the company, its suppliers, customers and regulators.
	They will search career sites for information about their role and what they can expect, they will review their job description and identify what tasks they think they will be expected to perform and how they will schedule these tasks during the week. They will look through their personal employment records for any certificates or documents about past achievements that relate to their new role.
Practically	Will get most of their information from doing their new job, but may also create additional practical experiences ahead of their start date by attending training courses or an induction session at the new company.
	Might ask questions at the interview about systems used or suppliers relevant to their work and will try to experience these before joining by learning new applications or visiting suppliers at exhibitions.
	Will be keen to do work as soon as possible in the 'live' environment so that they can gain an understanding of what is expected in their new role.
Reflectively	Wants to set their experience of taking a new job with this company in the context of others who have joined the company so may have questions for HR about other recent joiners or whether they will be assigned a buddy or a mentor for the first few weeks.
	Will seek out others who recently joined through social media or may ask their recruitment agency for details of anyone they have placed at this organization that they might be able to contact.
	Will search out online groups and associations of like-minded professionals and other members of their new organization. Will be keen to understand from others' experiences how long it has taken them to settle into their new role.

Emotional assessment

In order to form effective relationships it's important to understand the affect that you have on others, and consequently how others view us. This will influence how willing people are to form relationships with you and help clarify what they are expecting from the relationship.

Emotional assessment is formed of two elements: emotional triggers – an understanding of our emotional responses in different situations; and impact on others – an understanding of how our emotional state can affect the behaviour of others.

Emotional triggers

We face different situations every day at work, and they all have the capacity to trigger an emotional response. In order to manage the effects they have on us and others, we need to understand our likely responses to different situations. If there are situations that trigger positive responses then we should try to maximize these areas of work, and for those situations that trigger negative responses we should:

- aim to reduce the number of these situations we encounter;
- manage the situation so that our negative response is minimized;
- limit the impact that our negative response has on others.

Response questionnaire Understanding your emotional triggers means assessing your responses to different situations and understanding what has caused your reaction. Ask yourself the following questions.

For situations where you became angry or annoyed with yourself and/or others:

1 How did your frustration manifest itself?
- your ability to concentrate on the tasks;
- the speed at which you worked;
- the amount of effort that you put into your work;
- how you described your work to others;
- your attitude and demeanour.

2 What factors led to your frustration?

- limited belief in the benefits and meaning of what you were doing;

- insufficient level of autonomy or control you had;

- skills you were using:

  - type of work in which you have a high degree of competence;

  - skills that you were in the process of acquiring or had just been trained in.

- people you were working with:

  - familiar or unfamiliar;

  - from your organization or from other organizations.

- time pressure:

  - self imposed or defined by the situation;

  - unrealistic or not taking into account all aspects of the work involved.

- amount of experience you had in similar situations.

3 What could you have done to further improve the situation?

- asked for help from others;

- requested more time to remove some of the pressure from the situation.

For situations when you felt a genuine enjoyment for what you were doing:

1 How did your enjoyment manifest itself?

- the speed at which you worked;

- the amount of effort that you put into your work;

- how you described your work to others;

- your attitude and demeanour.

2 What factors affected your enjoyment?

- belief in the benefits and meaning of what you were doing;

- level of autonomy or control you had;

- skills you were using:
  - type of work in which you have a high degree of competence;
  - skills that you were in the process of acquiring or had just been trained in.
- people you were working with:
  - familiar or unfamiliar;
  - from your organization or from other organizations.
- time pressure:
  - self imposed or defined by the situation;
  - unrealistic or not taking into account all aspects of the work involved.
- amount of experience you had in similar situations.

3　What could you have done to further exploit the situation?

- trained others in what you were doing;
- explained the benefits of what you were doing to others.

Impact on others

You can use your self-assessment and emotional assessment to understand how you appear to others and how you can improve your engagement with others to increase the chances that they will want to follow your lead through the change. Engagement with others comes in two forms: direct and indirect.

Direct engagement　includes:

- face to face – when others can interpret your emotions through the words that you use, the tone of your voice and your facial expressions and other body language;
- on the telephone – when others can interpret your emotions through the words that you use and your tone of voice;
- in written communications – which might include e-mail or postings on social media sites where individuals can only interpret your emotions through the words that we use.

Case example

Ishan works for a large PR and advertising company, where he is responsible for sourcing images from photographic agents. He reports to the creative director who is very supportive and encouraging when Ishan wants to discuss work issues face to face, but appears uncaring and combative when he communicates with Ishan via e-mail.

This is because when the creative director writes e-mails, he does not include the 'softer' elements of the conversation that take place when he is discussing the issues face to face. His e-mails are written in a list style, setting out the tasks that must be completed to 'fix' the situation, whereas when he meets with Ishan he will acknowledge the difficulties and will even make jokes about the problems to lighten the atmosphere. This more relaxed approach is not reflected in his written style, and even though Ishan knows he means no harm, his e-mails imply impatience and anger about the situation which makes Ishan worry, and question whether he should have raised the issue in the first place.

Indirect engagement can be defined as how we are observed in our engagement with others – as this will be an indication of how we are likely to treat those that are observing us, and our attitude and behaviour which is observed as an indication of how we feel about the change.

Case example

Nikki has been working on a change initiative that is being sabotaged by the behaviour of her manager, Donna.

Donna would describe herself as being very open and honest and these are character traits that she is very proud of. The only problem within the context of the change is that she is very unguarded in what she says and who she says it to. In meetings and presentations that she attends as part of her business as usual responsibilities, she chats to people in other departments about how busy she is, how unwilling her staff are to implement the changes and how she is working long hours to try and get things implemented.

Donna doesn't realize that her negative comments spread fast around the company so when she holds her team meetings and praises her staff for their involvement in the change, it doesn't have the positive, motivational effect she is expecting. The result of her open and (too) honest behaviour is that her team don't think her praise is authentic and they judge her as untrustworthy – they know that in other situations she is saying the direct opposite about them.

Engaging with others For your engagement with others to have the greatest chance of success it's vital that you are able to put yourself in the other person's position and try to understand their perspective, so you can amend your approach to meet their needs. Consider these factors:

- Is this a subject that the other person feels territorial about – perhaps they see themselves as an expert in this subject or feel they have a lot of experience which should be acknowledged?
- Is this a subject that the other person has a history in – either a previous good or bad experience?
- Is this a subject that is very high on their personal agenda so they will have a great deal of interest in it?
- Is this subject of limited importance to the other person so they will have limited time to hear about the issue?
- Is the other person under a lot of pressure at the moment so will be quick to react negatively to any additional calls on their time?

Case example

Rita is incredibly enthusiastic about her work and is an acknowledged expert in her field, but fails to recognize that not everyone has her in-depth knowledge. In meetings, presentations and e-mails she jumps straight into the subject, expecting everyone she communicates with to respond immediately, ignoring the fact that her subject area is not top of their agenda or necessarily their favourite subject. She becomes frustrated when people do not provide her with the information she needs immediately and everyone else feels frustrated that she assumed that they would deal with her demands at the expense of their other work.

Below is a list of practical techniques that you can deploy to engage with people:

- Demonstrate your appreciation of their knowledge by referring to something they have been involved in and how it will be a useful contribution to the change.

- Align what you are saying to their positive experience by emphasizing the similarities with the change that you are proposing or acknowledge their previously negative experience by pointing out the differences to what is happening now.

- Do not present the situation as final. Reassure them that you want their participation and ask for their suggestions on how they would like to contribute.

- Be very specific about what you need them to do and how long you expect it to take. Do as much of the work as possible yourself. For example, if you are sending someone a document for review don't leave them to guess what sort of feedback you want. Create a feedback form with a handful of questions that relate to their specialist knowledge that it would be helpful to get their opinion about. This is demonstrating respect for how busy they are and the fact that they have knowledge no-one else has so there is relevance to asking them to get involved.

- Acknowledge that the change might not be high priority for them but explain why their response is high priority for you. For example, state that other work cannot be started without their contribution so that they can see you need a timely response.

Points to consider

Consider a recent difficult situation that you were involved in.

Review how you communicated the problem to others and identify what effort you made to understand their view and present the information in a way that best suited their needs.

Personal leadership

Personal leadership is the ability to control your responses to different situations by using your understanding of how you want to behave and overlaying this with an assessment of how best to behave to achieve your goals. It is about demonstrating self-control and using your understanding of how you behave to control your emotions and make sure your emotional response is relevant and proportional to the situation.

Personal leadership is formed of five elements:

- commitment;
- authority;
- self-control;
- trustworthiness;
- flexibility.

Commitment

As a change leader you are asking people to invest time and effort in learning new ways of working and developing new skills. You cannot expect them to fully participate if you do not show personal commitment to the same changes that you are asking others to make. You can demonstrate your commitment to the change in two ways.

Champion the change First, by championing the change, setting out a compelling case for why it is necessary and beneficial. It is hard for others to willingly participate in the change if those who are leading it do not appear to want it to happen. You must use all of the information acquired in defining the business need to answer the question 'what's in it for me?' so that others can see you have reconciled the need for the change and are comfortable with the situation.

The most disastrous change initiative I ever led was one that I thought was a waste of time. I had been told by my boss to transfer a number of processes and tasks from a team in New York to a team in London. Both teams were equally capable of doing the work; the New York team had good results and I could see no business benefits in transferring the work to London. In fact the transfer was part of a much wider reorganization that I was not informed about and simply couldn't find any enthusiasm for. I carried out my job but it was really hard work. Although I didn't say anything I was not my usual enthusiastic self and I didn't create any motivation for others to get involved. I eventually completed the transfer, but it took longer than it should have done, mainly because the lack of information and communication meant that the change wasn't a top priority for most people.

Change your behaviour

Second, by proactively making changes to the way in which you work to embody the changes and lead by example. People avoid those that they do not believe to be genuine or authentic. Why would others change how they work if you are not changing how you work? Making changes yourself will give you experience in the challenges and benefits of the change and this enables you to empathize with others.

Case example

Jurgen is the manager of a team of patent attorneys whose job is to review patent applications for their completeness before the application is submitted to the national patent office. To improve workflow and make use of new data mining software, all applications had to be reviewed and amended online. Previously all applications (which can be several hundred pages long) were printed, and the attorneys marked up their amendments which were later typed up by assistants. Jurgen had been doing this job for 30 years and was very comfortable with the old system. He understood the resistance of his team to the move to new technology as he was worried that staring at a screen and directly typing in amendments would be hard to get used to. He was also very aware that he would be taking the lead on this change project. He decided to start using the new technology on one of the applications he was supervising, and to write a blog letting his team know about his experiences. The blog described the successes and the problems he experienced, and how he overcame these problems with support from members of the IT team responsible for the system roll-out. The blog allowed Jurgen to share his feelings and demonstrate that he was having exactly the same experience as his team members.

Commitment involves prioritizing your work to be able to accommodate these additional activities so that they actually happen. It requires persistence in pursuing the change despite obstacles and setbacks. This type of commitment is commonly referred to as 'resilience'. Resilience is also the determination to see something through to its conclusion, even in the face of significant pressures. There are five elements to resilience:

Resilience factors

1 personal belief in your ability to handle unplanned events by reminding yourself how you have succeeded in these situations in the past;

2 creating an organized working environment that deals efficiently with planned work, leaving you with the energy and willingness to deal with unplanned events;

3 valuing your ability to deal with unplanned events by reminding yourself of how you have solved problems and created new solutions in the past;

4 recognizing that isolation from others removes you from a source of possible solutions and that accepting help from others is a positive response to setbacks;

5 accepting that your work is a balance of planned and unplanned events so your attitude must be a balance between organized and controlled, and flexible and open to new ideas.

Points to consider

In what ways do you demonstrate that you are personally committed to the change that you are involved in?

Authority

Our ability to inspire others to follow our lead is related to the amount of authority that others ascribe to us. We often associate authority with our position within the organization, and the authority we have over those that report directly to us. However, the ability to lead change cannot rely on this 'hierarchical' power because the change affects people in different functions and organizations that we do not control.

You have to develop authority through your knowledge, your personality and your presence. This means that you can take responsibility for leading the change wherever you are in the organization, and however little hierarchical authority you actually have, and you can achieve this by developing different types of authority.

Structural authority

This is hierarchical power, the authority you derive from the position you hold in the organization. This is often a mixture of job title, number of people that report to you, budgetary authority and the authority for commissioning work from others. There is very little you can do to grow this authority in the short term.

Specialist authority

This is the authority that is derived from the amount of knowledge and experience you have on a particular subject. It is the product of the qualifications that you hold, the recognition that you are the 'go to' person for solving problems, how often you are called upon to present your knowledge to others, perhaps through providing training and coaching in specialist aspects of your role, and how often your knowledge is referred to or sought out by others.

In the case of the change that you are trying to implement, your authority derives from your understanding of how the change will work and the differences that will exist between how work is conducted today and how it will be conducted after the change has taken place. No-one has any automatic authority in this area because the change is new and has created a situation that has not existed before. Therefore the level of authority you have will be a result of the amount of effort you put in to acquire specialist knowledge and demonstrate it to others.

A good way to build your specialist authority is by researching how the change has affected similar organizations. You can ask suppliers how they expect the change to impact the organization, convene discussions and workshops with colleagues to investigate the impact of the change, and form opinions and ideas.

Specialist authority is a product of hard work and needs to be publicized to others. It is not necessarily developed by being modest and hiding your accomplishments. It is enhanced through participation in other communities that are recognized as having expertise and specialist knowledge by your colleagues. You can join professional associations relevant to your job, and become a contributor to online forums.

Sinta is a junior manager in the finance department of a large utility company that recently implemented a new billing system. She says: 'Although senior management had been involved in deciding which new system to buy, no-one seemed to have much idea about how it would affect us. I had only recently been promoted so I was keen to show I knew what I was doing, so I did a lot of research. My team were extremely busy so I started briefing them for 10 minutes each week at our Team Meetings.

'I created a presentation pack with simple explanations of the changes and I showed clips of training videos I found on YouTube from other users of the system. The team found these sessions reassuring as they were learning that the new system was easy to use, and they were learning little and often which didn't detract from their other responsibilities.

'News of my information sessions spread quite quickly throughout the organization and I was asked to contribute to our internal website to keep everyone in the department up to date with the implementation. A lot of senior people noticed my work and asked me to present at their meetings. As a result my profile has risen and I am recognized outside of my department, which will be useful when I apply for my next promotion. My sessions have had a positive impact because they have created the impression that the new system is easy to understand and by learning about it in small pieces, the amount of new information does not feel overwhelming.'

Interpersonal authority

This type of authority is based on the ability to network and to derive power not from what we know but by being recognized as someone who knows who to contact. It is about building networks, recognizing when people have interests in common, when linkages between different groups would be a good idea and using the power of connections to make things happen. It involves being the orchestrator of contacts and support groups, rather than trying to force through all the work yourself.

Whilst some people have a natural affinity with others, interpersonal authority can be developed if you are prepared to work at it. It requires a willingness to share information with others and it involves listening skills to hear when people might need more information or would like to meet others in a similar situation. It necessitates memory and an ability to recall what others have said in the past that you can link to what someone is saying today.

Case example

Debra believes that her willingness to help others connect demonstrates her confidence in her own abilities. She says: 'I spend a lot of time helping others to connect with each other, sending introductory e-mails, summarizing their common interests or similar experiences to help them see the purpose for the connection. I respond to requests about whether I know someone who might be able to help with X as this builds my profile inside and outside the organization. It is nice to feel wanted and I get a real buzz when I attend industry events and realize how many people already know me or recognize my name.

'When I have to make changes to my ways of working, I have a lot of people that I can bounce my ideas off of, and lots of people that can give me a different perspective on the change and share their knowledge about how they would make the change happen.'

Physical authority

This is the authority that we derive from our presence and is indicated by our ability to gain and hold the attention of others. It is the product of body language and how we present ourselves to others. Some people believe that it is a product of charisma and cannot be developed – you either have this type of authority or you don't. I agree that some people naturally have high levels of physical authority or 'star quality' which means we automatically notice them in a room, and automatically notice what they are doing. However, you can improve your ability by thinking through how you come across, by being willing to speak up at meetings and events and to introduce ourselves to people you do not know.

In some meetings and presentations it is difficult to get people's attention because they are so busy catching up with each other – sometimes feel I am interrupting them! To increase my presence I make sure I get there early, I greet everyone at the door, and as people are taking their seats or getting a coffee I ask them about what they are expecting to hear and what questions they would like me to answer.

Points to consider

What is the strongest type of authority that you exhibit? What actions can you take to increase your level of authority in the other types?

Self-control

Self-control is your ability to restrain your natural reaction to a situation and substitute it with a more considered response. When we exhibit self-control we are making a conscious decision to push aside thoughts, feelings or actions and replace them with others that our personal awareness (self-assessment and emotional assessment) tells us would be more appropriate. In this way we are taking responsibility for our personal performance and managing the negative impact of our emotions on others.

During change there can be a lot of emotional responses driven by fear of the unknown and the stress of having to learn new ways of working. In this instance it's important to utilize your self-control to avoid reacting to these situations. A common example of the need for self-control is when someone hasn't done what they said they were going to do. A natural reaction is to get angry but this is not the most productive response as the other person is likely to become defensive and come up with reasons why the work couldn't be done on time and in turn you are likely to think these are excuses. On the other hand they might go on the offensive and blame you for not being clear about the deadline or what was expected. A controlled response to this would be to experience the anger in private. Say all the terrible things you want to say in your head and not out loud! Let the emotion pass before meeting with the person to work out how to fix the situation.

This self-control is particularly important in change situations as those we are working with are not under our direct control, and their involvement in the change has to be fitted around their other responsibilities.

Trustworthiness

Trust is an essential element of relationship building for change management. When you ask someone to change how they work, what you are actually asking them is to believe that doing things differently is the right thing to be doing, and that how they have been working before you came into the picture is now the wrong thing to do. It requires confidence in the new way of working which is a product of the person making the request to change as well as the logic of the changes themselves.

Trust has a direct impact on the speed in which change can take place, as shown in Figure 5.1. If there is trust then the person asked to change will accept what is being requested of them. If they do not have trust, they may still implement the changes but only after identifying, researching and assessing all of the possible options available to them, which will take time and delay the process of change.

Figure 5.1 Impact of trust on the speed of change

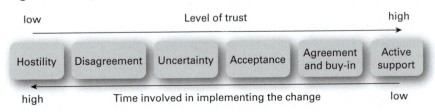

Bearing this in mind, it is counterproductive to rush into implementing a change without taking the time to create trust and build productive relationships. Without trust, those you need to implement the change will stand on the sidelines for longer, waiting to be convinced about the need for the change, the suitability of the changes and the reasons why they are beneficial. You will have to prove each point that you make about the change because people will be unwilling to accept what you say without evidence.

Trust is such an important subject that there is a large amount written about how to create it. After comparing over 20 different models of trust from a wide variety of sources, I suggest that the key elements to creating trust are:

Elements of trustworthiness

- be reliable – do what you said you were going to do, when you said you would do it;

- be predictable – be clear about your values and your positions on different issues so that others can understand your reactions to events;

- be congruent – make sure there is consistency between how you ask others to behave and how you behave yourself;

- be open – give honest feedback, do not avoid difficult conversations and welcome honest feedback in return;

- be loyal – give credit to others for their work and provide your support when it is needed.

Points to consider

Consider your relationship with a stakeholder for your change, where your engagement with this stakeholder began only recently.

How strongly are you exhibiting each of the five factors of trust?

What can you do to improve these levels?

Flexibility

When implementing change, the ideas and solutions that are needed will evolve over time as the environment into which we are implementing the change evolves and the results of some of our earlier ideas become apparent, which necessitates further changes. To be an effective change leader it's vital that you are comfortable with this emerging environment and remain open to new ideas. Your role is to identify and adopt change so you must be willing to seek out new opportunities and ideas. This flexibility requires a state of mind which recognizes that what you know today might not be what you need to know tomorrow so you must have a willingness to keep learning about the change: a willingness to welcome new participants to the change and a willingness to adopt new approaches or techniques.

Willingness to welcome new participants to the change New people bring a new perspective. Their understanding of the change is driven by their personality, their knowledge about the area being changed and their past experiences of change. Their new perspectives can lead to new requirements or new linkages between existing elements of the change.

Willingness to adopt new approaches or techniques Every change is different and there are no guarantees that a technique that worked well in a previous similar change will be appropriate for your change. Continue to ask for new suggestions throughout the life of the change and greet each new suggestion as a possibility worth investigating. This creates an open atmosphere which encourages people to speak up and share what they know without fear of censure or ridicule.

Developing personal leadership

Personal leadership does not happen by accident, it has to be planned. Think through what your responsibilities are and how you can best execute them so that you behave in a way that others will respond positively towards. Figure 5.2 shows a framework for assessing your current leadership ability and helps you to develop your leadership strengths for the change you are responsible for.

To complete the leadership framework:

- Create a description of the change that explains the scale of the work involved, the number and seniority of those impacted by the change within your organization and the seriousness with which the change will be viewed externally. Explain the purpose of the change and the benefits it is expected to deliver, along with the work that will be affected and the functions or departments that you will need to motivate to change.

- To identify your strengths and weaknesses, review the change capabilities index as shown in Appendix 5 to understand those aspects of the change that you feel able to manage and those where you need support.

Figure 5.2 Leadership framework

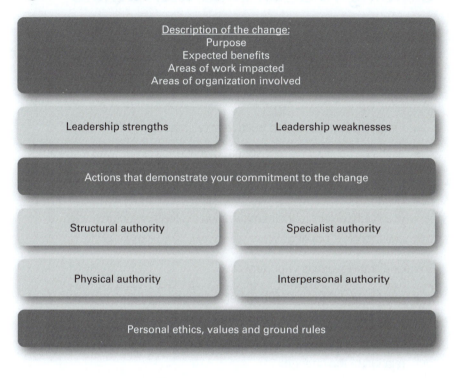

- For an idea of your responsibilities for the change and towards other people review the change activity index in Appendix 4.

- Review pages 165–69 for an understanding of the different types of authority and ask those that you trust to give you their opinion of the types of authority in which you have the highest leadership ability. Consider if there are any actions that you can undertake to increase your authority in relation to this change.

- Consider your personal values and establish any ground rules that you will want to adhere to during this change. For example, if you have a core value of respecting others, think through how this will affect how you explain the change to others and how you encourage them to participate in the change.

Building relationships with others

In order to build effective relationships with others you need to combine analytical thinking with the emotional intelligence derived from the personal awareness and personal leadership skills described in this chapter.

Analytical thinking is important to:

- identify who you need to build relationships with;
- assess what your current sphere of influence is and who else you need to include to help you implement the change;
- define what you need others to contribute to the change and how you might organize their contribution via team structures and collaborative working.

Emotional intelligence is important to:

- use the knowledge about ourselves to demonstrate empathy and build connections with others;
- appreciate the level of power and influence that others have in relation to the change;
- understand the different types of relationships that exist and how these apply to our change initiative.

This analytical and emotional thinking forms our empathy with others. The emotional intelligence developed through personal awareness and personal leadership helps us to develop empathy. Empathy is the understanding of another's situation, feelings, and motives and understanding of the emotional currents and power in relationships. It is created when we demonstrate that we are as interested in the concerns of others as we are about ourselves. Others will be willing to build a relationship with us if we are able to demonstrate our appreciation of how the change will affect them and we can involve ourselves in helping them to address their concerns.

Effective listening

We achieve this by using effective listening skills, which sounds easy but is difficult to do well in practice – in reality how many of us tend towards the column on the left in Table 5.3, instead of on the right?

Table 5.3 Non-empathetic and empathetic communication

Non-empathetic communication	Empathetic communication
Not listening to the response of the other person because you are waiting for your turn to speak	Allowing the other person to dominate the conversation, and not pushing forward your views
Not listening to the response of the other person because you are formulating your own thoughts and views	Willingness to reflect back the content and emotion of what you have heard from the other person so that you can check you have interpreted their perspective correctly
Listening to the response, but only retaining the information that supports your view and discarding the rest of the information	Remaining non-judgemental about what you have heard and not dismissing it as irrelevant or wrong
Asking questions that concentrate on finding out what the other person knows or believes, but not asking them why they hold these views or how they acquired their knowledge	Asking for an explanation of the source of their knowledge or reasons for their belief, to acquire an understanding of why and not just what
Judging the response that you get from the other person as right (accords with your views) or wrong (not aligned to your views)	Taking care not to interrupt and allowing the speaker to come to a natural close and complete the points they wish to make so that they feel they have been heard

The simplest way to understand what is important to another person is to ask, then *listen* to the answer. We all know when someone else is really interested in us. The other person is attentive, does not interrupt, does not fidget and does not speak about him or herself. This gives us time to think and feel accepted, rather than be judged. Listening leads to understanding; if you understand someone else fully, then you know what to do to get closer and work better together.

I used to work with someone who excelled at non-empathetic communication. We used to call her the steamroller because any conversation with her flattened anything in its path. I would leave our encounters knowing a great deal about how she felt about a particular change; what she saw as its benefits, its risks and how it was going to affect her, but knowing I had got very little of my own views across. She filled in every pause and every silence, she spoke in long sentences which were hard to interrupt. If I expressed any views not in agreement with hers she would bombard me with information until she had overridden what I had said. It was exhausting and pointless as I always had to follow up any encounter with an e-mail setting out my points.

Her behaviour slowed my ability to implement change as dealing with her took a disproportionate amount of my time.

Creating empathy

Empathy is an element of assertive behaviour – appreciating how others think and feel does not mean that your viewpoint is abandoned. Empathy isn't about agreeing with the other person, it is about acknowledging their perspective and combining it with yours to define an acceptable solution for both parties.

How do we know if we are acting with empathy? Ask yourself whether:

- There is genuine two-way contact with the other person – they seek you out as much as you seek them out.

- No subject is off limits – you believe that you can discuss anything with this person (in this context I am referring to work-related issues, not personal issues).

- You feel comfortable challenging the views that the other person expresses without feeling that your challenge would lead to a breakdown in your relationship.

- When you engage with this person you feel able to understand their perspective. You can recognize that it is perhaps different from yours and appreciate what those differences are.

- You are able to understand the reactions of the other person, their emotional state and show an appropriate response to it, either pleasure or concern.

- You trust what the person is saying to you and they trust what you are telling them so you do not need to identify or assess alternatives or contingency actions.

Without empathy it is difficult to form effective relationships as barriers will exist, for example:

- difficulty in getting access to people – we put off meeting or talking with those that we don't get on with;

- protecting our own interests – we are less likely to compromise or be willing to negotiate with someone who we feel doesn't understand our point of view;

- denial that there issues – it is harder to be honest about difficulties with those with whom we have no connection as we are afraid that they will form a poor opinion of us rather than support us;

- unwillingness to provide information or opinions – we are unsure of the reaction of those that we do not feel a connection with, so we restrict what we are willing to share;

- lack of confidence in challenging the opinions of others or defending our own position – without understanding the others' point of view we are more hesitant about saying what we really feel.

Points to consider

Consider your relationships with your stakeholders and identify those where you do not believe you have strong empathy.

Consider structuring your next meeting with them using the principles of empathetic communication.

Who to build a relationship with

In your role as change leader the purpose of the relationships you build is to generate the participation of everyone affected in making the change a reality and to establish yourself as a source of support and encouragement for those required to work in a new way so that once started on the change, momentum is maintained.

To use your time effectively you need to be clear about which relationships are going to be important to you and which relationships will affect how successful the change is. When we are implementing change we come across lots of people who need to be involved but aren't, those who are involved but don't need to be and those who are unaware that there is a change taking place (despite repeated attempts to let everyone know!).

The relationships that you may initially identify as being important to the success of the change are themselves subject to change as your ideas evolve. When the change is first conceived, and the impact on existing ways of working is understood, the scope of teams, departments, suppliers and customers etc will be identified.

However, as the change evolves to perhaps encompass more changes to processes, or to require the acquisition of new systems, the location, power, level of interest and volume of stakeholders will change. So relationship building must not be seen as a one-off activity, safely accomplished at the start of the change initiative. It requires continuous scanning of the environment, seeking out those that might not have been previously considered as integral to the change but who have a vital contribution which we can only access through an effective business relationship.

Of course the complexity is greater the bigger the organization that you are a part of. For those in smaller organizations where you meet all of your colleagues every day, you will not need to form new relationships but you may need to alter the basis of these relationships as you ask for additional effort during the life of the change initiative.

Case example

Shona is the finance manager for a professional association which employs 67 people. When she began the replacement of the organization's finance systems she soon realized that she would need to redefine a lot of her relationships. Although she has quite a lot of responsibility and reports directly to the managing director, many people knew her as the lady who sorts out their expenses! Getting people to relate to her in her role of change manager meant demonstrating her authority and her power. This has been especially important in re-defining the relationships she has with other managers whose departments need to change to fit with the new financial processes.

Identifying potential relationships

This section of the book may feel quite analytical, and I am not suggesting you categorize the usefulness or relevance to the change of everyone that you meet. However, by applying some of the techniques described below you are less likely to miss out the obvious and make your work more difficult by ignoring someone that you should have involved from the beginning.

So, key steps are:

- scan your horizon and identify as many change participants and impacted individuals as possible;

- categorize them in some way so that you can understand the type of relationship you might have with them;

- understand how much influence you have and when it would be better to involve others to build relationships and encourage participation in the change.

Scan your horizon

In Chapter 4 we looked at creating a community map to help identify those impacted by the change. To be effective it must be regularly reviewed. To decide what will trigger a review, consider:

- specific points in the roadmap when elements of the change have been delivered;

- a regular schedule, eg weekly or monthly;

- ad hoc additions and amendments to your community map following suggestions from other stakeholders.

Categorize the possible relationships according to the impact of the change

To keep things simple consider using three groups (Figure 5.3):

- impacted – those who are involved directly with the work that is affected by the change;

- affected – those that make use of the work that is affected by the change or supply inputs to this work;

Figure 5.3 Relationship categories

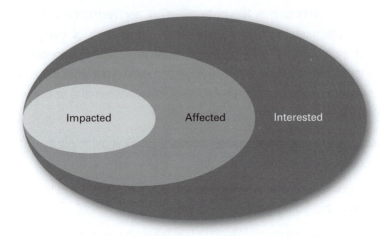

- Interested – those not directly affected by the changes but who have an interest in the impact of the change on the strength and capability of the organization.

Impacted Identify the people that are directly affected by the change by looking at your work end to end, for example those who:

- provide the inputs that enable you to do your work;
- create or own the processes that you apply to your work;
- authorize your work as complete;
- are the recipients of the outputs of your work;
- audit your work to ensure it is being done correctly.

Affected Identify those affected by identifying the inputs and outputs and their sources, for example those who:

- supply information or other resources in order for you to complete your work;
- are recipients of information and data created by your work;

- are users of tangible products and services created as a result of your work;
- need to know that work in your area is being completed to agreed quality standards and service level agreements.

Interested Identify those with a 'whole organization' viewpoint who regard your change as part of their success, for example those who:

- are responsible for the public relations message;
- analyse the results of your company on behalf of investors and regulators;
- are in senior positions in your organization who use the results of your changes as an input to their decision making;
- are in senior positions in other organizations who use the results of your changes as an input to their buying or hiring recommendations.

For each of these groups, try to understand their areas of connection and shared interest with you:

- What are they trying to accomplish?
- Who do they have to report to?
- What are their key areas of responsibility?
- How can you help them and how can they help you?
- What is the current state of your relationship? Positive, neutral or negative?

(I have given another example of how to categorize those impacted by change in the section on 'Levels of engagement' on pages 182–83).

Irrespective of how you identify who you have to build relationships with, the list will contain those who support the change, those who oppose it and those who are indifferent. We need to build an environment that encourages participation in the change (see Chapter 6).

My advice on how to build relationships is to understand who that person reports to and what kind of relationship they have with their boss. If they are being closely managed then I can help them by giving them information about the change in a formal way, maybe via a regular report which they can pass onto their boss without having to do any extra work. If they have a good relationship with their boss and there is a lot of trust between them then I can involve them in advocating the change and I know they will be listened to.

My tip for building effective relationships is to ignore the hierarchy and make friends at all levels and in all areas of the organization. It is a cliché to say that the receptionist or the PA is the person who knows the most about the company but it became a cliché because it is true.

Levels of engagement

The strength of your relationship is based on the empathy you create, which is driven by your ability to understand the views and perspectives of others. Your ability to appreciate the views of others will in part be determined by the amount of common ground that you share with the other person and the amount of information that you are allowed to share. This is affected by the position that the person holds within your organization. For example, I have identified four positions that affect how we relate to others (Figure 5.4).

Local colleagues

The amount that you have in common with those that work in the same organization as you and are co-located with you is naturally greater than with those who work for a different organization. As you work for the same

Figure 5.4 Levels of engagement

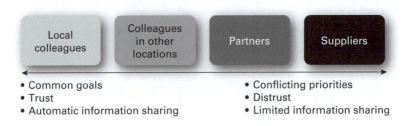

organization you will have common goals and your work will be assessed and governed using common performance metrics and standards. There are likely to be few, if any, barriers between you for sharing information, which will be made easier because you use common systems. You are likely to have knowledge of each other's daily routine, likes and dislikes and share similar experiences of office life which provides you with a basis for developing further knowledge about each other.

Colleagues in other locations

Some colleagues may be based in other offices or may work from home. Building relationships with these colleagues has all the advantages of those you are co-located with in terms of shared systems and processes but there may be some distance between you because you lack a common physical location.

Partners

Partners are those that we work with who are employed by another organization but are assigned full time to working for our organization via outsourcing arrangements. These individuals use the same systems and procedures as ourselves but there may be restrictions on the type of information that we can share with them. There may also be barriers between us because they report to different line managers, are incentivized differently and have different options for training and career development.

Suppliers

We may work very closely with individuals based in supplier organizations, who will be just as affected by the change as we are. However, as they are employed by a different company and have a responsibility to sell their products and services to our organization they will not share common strategic goals. There will be barriers to the amount of information that we can share with them.

Groups versus individuals

Another factor that affects our relationships is our ability to understand the differences that exist between one-to-one and group relationships:

- In one-to-one relationships it is common for people to compare their levels of power with each other and allow the seniority and position of power to flow between each other as the issue is discussed.

- In team environments individuals have their own power, but also a level of power that results from the role that they perform within the team. For example, if you are raising issues about what needs to change with someone one to one, you will both evaluate each other to ascertain your knowledge, power and commitment to the change – you will use this to decide how much you want to compromise and how much you want the other person to compromise. If you are meeting this person as part of a team affected by change, your decisions on how much you are prepared to flex your position can be hampered by that person's need to maintain their power within the team. Whilst, of course, relationships aren't about conflict, as effective change managers you do have to recognize that these power plays exist.

Points to consider

Consider how recently you created your community map or analysis of your stakeholders.

Have there been significant points of progress in your change since this time?

Have there been amendments to the scope or expected deliverables of the change?

If so, update your list of your stakeholders and re-analyse their categories as these may have changed as your change has evolved.

Steps in building relationships

Building relationships with others is not a linear process. Relationships are the product of multiple interactions, both planned and unplanned. However, there are some steps that you can take to speed up this process.

Make people aware of who you are and what you know

If you are going to form a relationship with someone then they first need to be aware that you exist and to appreciate the value that engaging with you might offer them. To form relationships with all those impacted by change you should begin with those already in your network, and then use these connections to establish your presence with others with whom you have had no previous engagement.

A network is a group of interconnected people who interact to exchange information and knowledge. Networks are powerful because we can use them to connect with people we do not come across as we carry out our everyday activities, and enable us to access the knowledge and skills of others quickly.

A network requires contacts and a willingness to help these contacts form connections by realizing their shared or complementary interests and goals. Members of a network trade value with each other, where that value is the acquisition of knowledge, access to expertise or the ability to influence someone in the direction you want them to move. To be an effective member of a network you need to be clear about what you are able to offer, ie making a case for why someone should connect with you by establishing your knowledge and experience, and to be willing to continually enhance the value of the network by contributing new information and experiences, introducing new members and linking existing members to form new relationships.

As the basis of your relationships with others, you need to ensure that being connected to you is a positive experience for others. Relationships require energy and those that you want to engage with will be assessing the value that you offer to see if a relationship with you is worthwhile. My favourite quote on this is from Liz Wiseman in her book *Multipliers*, who believes that when you are positioning yourself to build connections between people you should see yourself in the position of 'genius maker', whose role is to 'amplify the smarts and the capabilities of other people'.

For example, I always make sure I introduce myself to anyone I don't know at a meeting or an event. So if I think there are going to be new people there I will turn up early and leave some space in my diary afterwards so I have time to chat. I also follow up with a future invitation to a similar event or to arrange a lunch to get to know them better.

Connection maps

In our network we will have a number of people with whom we have strong affinity, those that we know through 'friends of friends' and those that we used to know well and had active connections with which have lessened in the last few years.

In Figure 5.5 my connections surround me, with strong ties to my active connections and my other connections acting as a satellite around me, if I choose to make contact or if they choose to contact me.

Whilst I have the strongest relationship with my active connections, they are likely to be in the same work groups as me, and we probably have a number of connections in common. The reason I made such a strong connection with them is probably because we share similar views or perspectives.

Whilst these people are likely to be impacted by the same change as me, they are by no means the only ones impacted. There will be lots of people in other networks that are affected by the change and whose cooperation I will need in order for the changes I make to the way I work to be accepted and incorporated into how my organization works internally and how it engages suppliers and customers externally.

So I need to reach out to others. The counterintuitive issue is that the best way to reach out to others is not via my active connections but through those who I have a weaker relationship with, because they are more likely to have the contacts I need and can act as a bridge between my tight inner circle of colleagues and connect me to the wider world.

Sleeper connections are probably easier to contact because there is already a shared history or past connection that can be referred to, and as they were a connection in the past there will be some trust between us.

Figure 5.5 Connections map

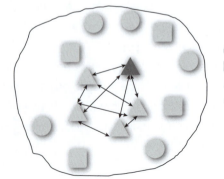

Key
Loose connection
Inactive (sleeper) connection
Active connection
Me

Figure 5.6 Detailed connections map

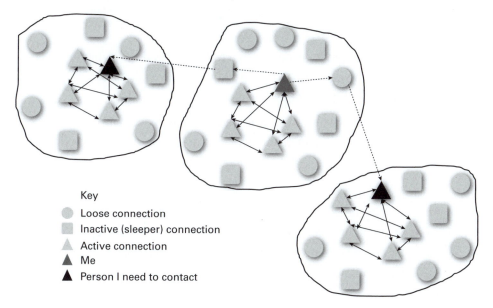

Key
- Loose connection
- Inactive (sleeper) connection
- Active connection
- Me
- Person I need to contact

Looser connections are harder to engage with because I haven't yet formed a strong relationship with them. I may have met them in passing or know of them through someone else, but I am going to have to fight through shyness and contact them so that they can help me reach the person I need in their network.

I will have to be prepared to 'exchange value' in order to acquire these additional connections. Value equates to providing help, information or introductions to these looser connections in exchange for them introducing me to their active connections.

Creating connections

Once introduced I need to employ my emotional intelligence and empathy to form the relationship, moving through a number of stages:

- Being the provider of information – in the initial stages of the relationship, I am providing a one-way stream of information that hopefully will attract the attention of the other person and make them interested to learn more. I need to employ empathy to ensure that I put these messages across in a way that acknowledges their perspective and is as relevant to their interests and priorities as possible.

- Being viewed as a source of value – hopefully this information will generate a willingness to engage with me, requesting more information about the change.

- The next step is taking part in a two-way exchange of information where the person is willing to share their views and knowledge and work together to create greater understanding.

- As a result of this two-way engagement, responsibility for the change passes from me to the other person as they become involved in the change and begin to take ownership of their own change activities.

Initially the person might be willing to engage with me because of the respect they have for the person that introduced us. Although the change that I am responsible for is very important to me it may appear irrelevant to the other person, but they will give me an opportunity to make my case. My ability to build rapport with this person and develop links between us enables me to change their perspective so that they no longer view the change as something that I am doing but as something that they want to take responsibility for.

Points to consider

Review all of the meetings you attended in the last week, the e-mails you have sent and other communications you have been involved in.

How many of these brought you into contact with new people?

Have you pursued further contact with those with whom you don't have existing relationships? Consider identifying additional people that you need to contact to explain your change or ask for their experiences of change.

Bring all of these connections together to form change teams

To successfully implement change, all those affected have to decide for themselves that they are prepared to work differently and to identify and adopt these changes. To provide support for this effort, we should encourage our connections to form into self-directed change teams.

A change team is a very fluid construct because many members do not choose to become a member of a team; their membership is a product of the impact that the change is having on them. So although you may be working with this group of people, they may not see themselves as a formal team but as a group of like-minded individuals.

Effective teams have a shared common purpose that is understood and agreed by every team member, irrespective of their different perspectives on how this purpose should be achieved. The result of the work carried out by the change team is to enable each individual team member to create their own new way of working and make the change a reality for them. So it is important that within the shared goals, individual perspective is maintained.

Each team member has to push themselves through the emotional transition of learning to work differently (see Chapter 6). This push will come from their own motivation for change. To enable change team members to generate intrinsic motivation for participating in the change, you need to:

- clarify the contribution and value of organizing individuals into a change team, and encourage each team member to define the value of their contribution;

- ensure that the team is small enough that each individual can have autonomy over the work that they do, without having to operate within a larger team hierarchy;

- enable team members to play to their strengths and decide for themselves the type of work that they do and the contribution that they make;

- help team members choose their contribution by clearly articulating all of the work that needs to be accomplished to make the change a reality, as well as articulating the order in which some of these tasks should be carried out (see Chapter 6).

Self-directed teams

These success criteria have been adopted by those that describe effective teams as self-directed teams. Self-directed teams are different from teams that are established as part of a command and control structure in that they do not wait to have their work distributed to them by a central organizer but instead take responsibility for defining, scheduling and executing their own workload.

Self directed teams are appropriate for implementing change because your hierarchical authority as the change leader is limited. The change team will contain members from different functions, with different levels of personal authority and may even come from different organizations. However senior you are in your organization you are unlikely to be 'in charge of the team'.

Self-directed teams have the following characteristics:

1 they ask questions and clarify their understanding of the work;
2 they require minimal direct supervision;
3 they are empowered to take decisions about how to prioritize their work;
4 they take decisions about resources and the allocation of tasks;
5 they communicate continuously with other members of the team and take responsibility for keeping each other informed of progress;
6 they contribute innovative ideas and improvements about their work and the work of other team members;
7 they have collective ownership of the work that the team delivers;
8 they take responsibility for developing their own skills;
9 they have a high degree of interest in their work.

Effectively the team 'self organizes' its work. If the team members are given the opportunity to select work that matches their core skills then this will increase their intrinsic motivation and provide momentum within the team. This self-direction relies on individuals being empowered to take decisions. Empowerment requires clear boundaries establishing to what extent an individual can decide what to change, how long to take and how much money to spend etc, and coaching to give them the confidence to take their own decisions and not to look to others to organize their work.

Coordinating self-directed teams – self-directed teams are driven by
regular coordination of the work rather than detailed planning and scheduling of the tasks. This approach aligns well with the agile approach to change. As more becomes known about the change, new tasks will be identified which the team will distribute amongst its members. This makes the team more productive than one with strong reliance on a central plan because it saves time: time is not taken up producing detailed plans and schedules at the start of the change initiative; and time is not required to re-plan the work every time the change evolves and new tasks are identified.

As the change leader your role is not the day-to-day management of the team resources or the administration of the team processes. Instead, your role is to maintain the motivation of the team by removing any obstacles to their progress. These obstacles will include:

- lack of resources to undertake tasks or review and test the quality of the work being done by the team;
- delays by suppliers;
- misunderstandings about scope, purpose or required features and functions;
- changes to personnel in the operating environment in which the change will be implemented;
- actions of competitors, regulators or other organizations that affect the market (commercial organizations) or community (public sector organizations) in which the change is being delivered.

To prevent delays, these potential 'roadblocks' should be identified and removed before they are experienced by the team. This means:

- high-quality risk analysis that assesses every aspect of the change, the operating environment that it is being implemented into and the demands of the market or community;
- proactive 'horizon scanning' to identify and manage conflicts of interest, initiatives that will compete for the same resources and the progress of activities upon which our change is dependent.

Power law distribution As so many people are impacted by change and will have a need to participate in the work of the change team at some point in the lifecycle of the change, it is important that team membership welcomes contribution from everyone. These contributions are driven by the power law distribution (Figure 5.7).

Figure 5.7 Level of contribution

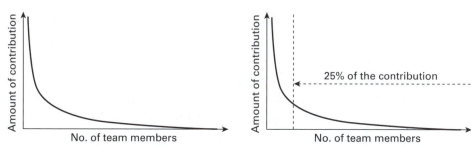

This maps the contribution of team members and recognizes that for a myriad of reasons some members will contribute a great deal more than others, but that membership should not be restricted to those that are likely to contribute the most. In change, we need everyone to participate so we must create structures that enable everyone to make their contribution, whatever the size of that contribution.

In the power law distribution, the top 10 per cent of the contributors contribute 75 per cent of the effort, whilst the remaining 25 per cent of the effort is spread across contributions from the other 90 per cent of the team. Effectively the curve states that the tenth member of the team will only contribute 10 per cent of the amount that the highest contributor contributes, and the one hundredth member of the team will only contribute 1 per cent of the work that the top contributor undertakes. However, for our change team to be effective we need this 1 per cent of effort because it is this 1 per cent that could be the small change that ensures that the change is effective.

As everyone in the team has a need to make amendments to their own ways of working, it is important that there is sufficient autonomy for team members. So whilst the potential membership of the change team is very large, it is best managed as a series of smaller change teams where individuals can demonstrate their personal leadership capability without being overwhelmed or demotivated by the number of individuals with whom they have to collaborate at any one time.

Case example

Over the last few months I have been watching how a change team in a local charity has been preparing for a move to a bigger office on the other side of town. There has been a small core of very active members who have visited the new site, drawn up floor plans, decided on allocation of offices and identified which teams will sit where. The majority of the team members have given feedback when it has been asked for but have not been very proactive. Two members of the change team (Jeff and Imran) are on the periphery. They have not carried out any work in relation to the change and have not provided any feedback on the work of others. However, last week Jeff gave one of the core team the details of an interior designer who is a big supporter of the charity and is willing to help source carpets and desks at cost. Jeff's contribution 'came out of nowhere' and since then he has blended into the background again, but the result of his contribution will be a considerable cost saving for the charity.

Encourage collaborative working

It is vital for all members of the change team to work together as there is so much interdependence between processes, systems and information. One of the principles of good change management is to constantly assess each change for its ability to create unintended consequences. It is only by working together and having access to all information about the change that we can address these knock-on effects and make amendments to minimize their disruption or make everyone aware of them to maximize the opportunities they offer.

Collaboration is a general term derived directly from the Latin words for 'working together'. It means organized sharing and in a change team that means shared responsibility for:

- achieving understanding about the impact of the change and what is required to make the change a reality;

- sharing ideas to create an innovative environment that enables new ways of working to be created;

- completing tasks and making sure that all the work necessary to implement the change has been completed irrespective of who originally agreed to do it and who actually does it.

The benefits of collaborative working are:

- that it increases the quality of the solution because it has been evaluated from a number of different perspectives;

- that it provides an environment for continuous transfer of knowledge as the participants share their knowledge with each other;

- the speed of creation as people work together so they do not need to wait whilst others review their work;

- that it accesses a wide range of knowledge and skills across all team members, reducing the need to hire other specialists;

- that it increases the likelihood that problems will be solved because the solution is not the sole responsibility of one individual but involves the contribution of team members;

- that it increases the likelihood that work will be completed because resources can be easily transferred between tasks so nothing remains undone.

Success criteria for collaborative working

Cultural factors:

- relationship building is a priority and is encouraged at all levels of the organization;
- information sharing is encouraged and silo based working is discouraged;
- innovation is supported by quality standards to ensure that outputs meet organizational needs;
- individuals are respected for their knowledge and expertise irrespective of their position within the organization;
- there is an appreciation for ideas generation and recognition that the best solutions are a product of many ideas;
- there is a high degree of trust that ideas will be treated with respect.

Personal factors:

- there is a willingness to suspend judgement when ideas are being shared until everyone has had a chance to absorb the information;
- individuals willingly give credit to each other for their contribution;
- people make time for collaboration and balance their work between individual tasks and collaborative effort.

Conclusion

Committing energy and skill to making change a reality is an emotional decision, in part driven by the opinions of our peers, and the opportunities to work alongside those we respect and to develop relationships with new people from who we can learn new skills.

The quality of the relationships you build with those impacted by change will determine the success of your change. Effective relationships are built on empathy and trust and are robust enough to allow for proposals to be debated and challenged to produce a better outcome.

Environment

06

Introduction

Environment is the atmosphere, working conditions and community of colleagues and contacts in which we work. It is a significant determining factor on our ability. The environment in which you operate can help you:

- design and create relevant and appropriate changes;
- successfully implement change;
- continue to support the changes until they are embedded as the new 'business as usual'.

I work with a lot of executives who recognize the competitive advantage of creating this environment which they often refer to as the capability for change, or change management maturity. There are no easy definitions of what this capability involves, but it is often described as an ability to integrate continuous change into working practices whilst maintaining a focus on business as usual. This capability for change incorporates a belief that change initiatives are not special, one-off events but are an essential facet of every role. Everyone, whatever their job has a responsibility to lead and/or participate in change so that activities and processes are continually improved and that the concept of business as usual, as it applies in your organization, continually develops to meet your customers' expectations.

Five activities are commonly mentioned when people describe how they are developing this capability:

- continually scanning the horizon for new ideas, assessing their potential value and selecting those with the greatest business value;
- assessing existing working practices for obsolescence and stopping anything that does not add value without blame or recrimination on those who originally instigated the practice;

- having a shared view across all functions within the organization of the importance of continuous enhancement and improvement;
- seamlessly implementing change into existing working practices as part of a process of constant renewal;
- being part of a team that views change as part of the day job and not something different or extra to their current role.

In this chapter we will look at the factors needed to establish an environment that reassures, encourages and motivates those involved in change.

Setting the scene

Throughout this book I have taken a pragmatic view of managing change. We are all judged on short-term, visible results so I have confined my guidance on the environment for change to meet the needs of the change you are involved with, and not to attempt to create the wider organizational capability for change that I have just described. If you are successful in creating an environment that helps your change to thrive then your success can be replicated in other change initiatives, but first you need to define an environment that:

- aligns to your organization's mission, vision and values;
- supports an agile approach;
- is relevant to the changes you are expected to make.

Environment and its links to organizational culture

Every organization has a prevailing culture that is formed over time, and is a product of the values and activities of the organization, the markets in which it operates and the behaviours and attitudes of those that work for the organization.

Culture defines our engagement with the organization at the high level, including:

- pride in our work;
- how valued we feel when we are at work;

- how comfortable we feel in expressing our views to our colleagues and our superiors;
- the range and depth of relationships that we form with our colleagues;
- the level of trust and satisfaction we portray about our organization to customers and suppliers;
- what we wear to work;
- how we talk to those we work with and for;
- how we prioritize our work;
- our willingness to do more than the minimum required of us.

Changes that align to your existing culture will have a natural level of support whilst those that work against what already exists will be met with resistance. This is not to say that as change leaders we should not implement changes that go against how things are currently done, but we do need to think about how much push back we are likely to encounter.

It is commonly accepted that organizational culture is the most difficult attribute to change. It remains constant even when the people, the location and the products and services of the organization change. Culture is very 'sticky'. We can create short-term shocks that change it temporarily but in many cases it returns to the status quo (Figure 6.1).

Figure 6.1 Factors that maintain the current culture

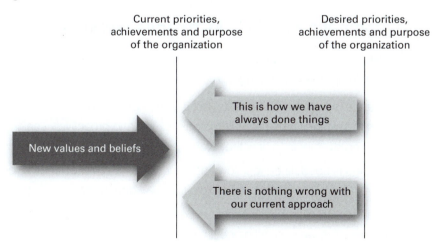

For cultural change to have any effect a large-scale transformation programme to redefine an organization's culture would need to take place, taking several years and involving the restructure of purpose, people and process. Therefore, it is important to take a pragmatic view and narrow the scope of the effect you can reasonably expect to have on the culture if you are to have any success with a specific change initiative.

If you are able to accept that, for the purposes of your change, it is not possible to redefine the culture of the organization, you can focus on creating an atmosphere that is supportive of change in your area and actively encourages the adoption of new ways of working. The environment in which you work is a small subset or mini version of your organization's culture, but a subset over which you have control.

Building the right environment relies on leading by example. You can decide how you will behave by selecting the values, behaviours and attitudes that you think will best encourage people to implement the change. You can decide what behaviours in others you will encourage and celebrate, and which behaviours you will actively discourage. Your embodiment of these behaviours will affect your ability and that of your colleagues to successfully implement change. Your environment grows as a result of a virtuous circle: as you choose to behave a certain way you will seek out others who you think are sympathetic to your approach; as others see you behaving in a way that matches their own beliefs then they will seek you out and join forces with you. (See Chapter 5: Relationship building, on how your self-management is an essential component of creating a supportive environment.)

Environment and its links to agile working

The environment that you create has to recognize key factors associated with an agile approach to change:

- change is not a one-off activity, but it is the normal state so everyone has to split their time between doing their job and proactively seeking out improvements to how they work;

- change is not defined top down and everyone has a responsibility for identifying improvements and exploiting new opportunities;

- change is constant, so we must expect repeated iterations of change altering how we work all of the time;

- change is uncertain as the solution continues to evolve, and we are not working on a pre-defined, pre-planned initiative that is known in detail from the start;

- change is the product of collaborative working where there are no restrictions on sharing information and trying out new ideas.

This means that you need to clarify a number of issues that guide how you approach change. First of all, it's important to be very clear and unambiguous about the expected outcomes, so that everyone involved will be able to undertake activities that contribute to the change and help monitor progress as well as warn those leading the change if they think it is going off course.

As there are so many people involved in the change, it is important to decide how decisions will be made, and how issues and conflicts will be addressed. This gives those involved belief that there is a fair and equitable process underpinning your approach which leads them to trust you as their change leader. These decisions will include a definition of how much autonomy individuals impacted by change will have for making changes to their ways of working, and when their ideas will have to be escalated to those leading and sponsoring the change for authorization.

For changes expected to take a considerable amount of time to implement, it is important to decide how to measure the contribution of all those involved so that the time they spend involved in the change is recorded as part of the performance management process. It is difficult for individuals to choose to participate if their change efforts are not recognized on a par with their efforts to carry out their business as usual responsibilities. This recognition needs to extend to the redrafting of job descriptions to reflect the need to balance doing the work with improving the work.

To help you create an environment that supports your change, consider your approach, your authority and your ability (Figure 6.2). Assess these three interrelated factors against your current working environment and identify what information needs to be clarified and what decisions need to be taken to establish an environment that supports your change.

Approach

This describes the work ethic, level of seriousness and commitment that you want people to demonstrate when they are participating in change. Points to consider include:

Figure 6.2 Elements of your environment

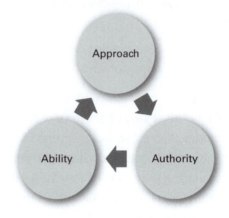

- Is remote working to be encouraged? If so, how will those not co-located with their colleagues be included in information sharing and problem-solving sessions?
- Is time to be allocated to the change activities in large blocks or fitted around business as usual activities?
- Are those involved given instruction in the activities they must undertake or are they asked to decide for themselves how to manage the changes they are making?
- How will successes and failures be recognized?

Authority

This describes the level of empowerment that exists for each person involved in the change. Considerations include:

- Are individuals formally assigned to change roles?
- How will people decide which actions they are responsible for?
- How will individuals notify other colleagues of their areas of responsibility?
- In what circumstances might formal delegation of work be appropriate?
- Under what circumstances must issues and risks be escalated to more senior managers and when can they be managed by those individuals impacted by them?

Ability

This describes the technical and interpersonal skills needed to implement the change. Considerations include:

- What are the core skills that are needed to make this change happen?

- Are there any gaps between the capabilities of those involved in the change and the required skills?

- If so, are these gaps to be filled via training or the hiring of additional, skilled resources?

- How is knowledge of what works and what doesn't to be communicated during the change?

Points to consider

Does your current working environment encourage you and your colleagues to take responsibility for change?

Are you clear about your level of autonomy when leading change?

Do you think that everyone impacted by change is clear about how they can participate in its creation?

Environment needs to provide reassurance

It is important to create a supportive environment if people are to overcome their natural resistance to change. Overcoming resistance is important because everyone must become their own change agent. New ways of working involve everyone, from the person who makes significant changes to how they work and the outputs they create, to those who are the recipients of these new outputs who have to change their work to accommodate them. Therefore, involving only a few people in making change happen is doomed to failure. The people involved in changing their ways of working will form their own sub-group, supporting each other and learning to adapt to the new ways of working. Those outside of this sub-group will continue to work in the old ways, leaving a two-tier system that is incapable of achieving the benefits of the change.

Reactions to change

Our reactions to change are not logical, they are emotional, based on past experiences of change, satisfaction with the status quo, fondness for change as a concept and concern about what will be expected of us in the new business environment and whether we have the skills and capabilities to thrive in these new ways of working. This emotional reaction will govern how much resistance there will be; if you are to lead yourself and others through change effectively, it is important to understand what drives this reaction so that you can provide the necessary support and encouragement to adopt new ways of working.

Prior to the change, we carry out many activities almost unconsciously, automatically and without having to think about them. This is because they have become habits, automatic reactions to how we behave in certain situations. When you arrive at work, you probably have a routine set of tasks that you carry out, probably doing several things at once because some of these tasks are so normal that they are happening in the back of your brain. You are not consciously thinking them through because you do them every day. For example, you might take off your coat, switch on your computer, say hello to your colleagues without looking up from your desk; search through your bag for some papers, look at the clock and decide how long you have before you need to leave for a meeting and decide that you want a drink.

Now imagine that when you arrived at work today you had to go to a different desk because there was an office move yesterday and you have been re-located. You have to think about where your new desk is, you want to take off your coat but you are not sure where to put it anymore so you decide to keep it on for a few minutes. You look around you to see who your nearest neighbours are, and engage them in conversation, giving them your full attention because they are new to you and you are putting in some effort to form a relationship with them. You sit down at your new desk and familiarize yourself with what is on it and where everything is placed. You switch on your computer and then look around you to see if there is a wall clock. You think through the journey from your new desk to the meeting location and start to calculate if you have time to get a drink before you have to leave for the meeting.

A simple change can have a big impact on how you feel. In the second example you will feel more stressed and less confident than in the first example. We instinctively know this is true so we resist change because it disturbs our comfortable world.

When people are told about future changes, they begin the process of adjustment or transition to the new reality. Often the first reaction is shock, even if you knew the change was likely to happen. Shock might seem a strong reaction to a change at work, but it is the product of concerns about our ability to cope, which manifests itself in a number of fears:

- we are concerned about how much knowledge and experience we are losing;
- we are not sure if the new way of working will be more difficult, more time consuming than what we have today;
- we fear being left behind as others adapt to the changes more quickly than we do;
- we are worried about how hard it will be to learn something new.

These fears develop as people move through five reactions to change

1 appreciating the current state;
2 loss of group membership;
3 learning new things;
4 loss of productivity;
5 appreciating the new state.

As a change leader it's vital that you provide reassurance to your colleagues by empathizing with them so that they feel confident enough to address their concerns and overcome them.

Appreciating the current state

For this reason, some resistance to change manifests itself in an appreciation for what we have today. When people know they are losing something it becomes more valuable, and even if the system or processes they use today cause lots of problems, they are more likely to overlook these issues and think about what the advantages are. This can slow down our willingness to embrace the change because we are judging the future unfairly, using a very positive view of the present to compare it against, which means we are more likely to see the change in a negative light.

You can help this process by giving very clear messages about what the future working environment needs to include, and what aspects from the existing ways of working will not form part of this future. Whilst this may appear confrontational, this very clear signposting of what is and is not important can give people who are struggling to assimilate the changes 'permission' to abandon the old ways of working, which frees up space for them to adjust to the new ways of working.

Loss of group membership

Another fear that drives resistance to the change is about being left behind or being left out. In the way we work today we are part of many informal groups, based upon our knowledge and what we contribute at work. One person might be known for their ability to fix the current system when files become corrupted and data is lost, or there might be someone who knows why an extra form is used for customer enquiries alongside the standard procedures. So people turn to them when their knowledge is needed and useful. Losing these relationships and having to reform them, perhaps with different knowledge or with an entirely different group of people, makes them nervous. They worry about their value in these new groups and how they will be perceived by others.

Learning new things

People are also worried about their ability to learn new things. Everybody knows that learning something new is hard. It takes a lot of effort and concentration. Levels of activity will increase as people try to process new information whilst at the same time continuing to carry out business as usual responsibilities (Figure 6.3).

If people are already very busy at work they naturally wonder how they are going to find time to acquire this new knowledge. It's also common for people

Figure 6.3 Level of activity during change

to worry about whether they can learn as fast as others, or whether they will be seen as falling behind, and therefore less useful. If someone is in a position of authority they might worry about how the respect that others have for them will be damaged by having to admit they don't have any experience in the new ways of working, so they are on the same level as everyone else.

Everyone has a different threshold for change, ie the amount of change they can cope with before they become overwhelmed by it. These thresholds are affected by the amount of immunity that the person has built up based on the amount and type of change they have experienced in the past. This can include work related change and personal change. If someone has had the same job, at the same location and with many of the same colleagues for a number of years whilst at the same time they have lived in the same house, with the same partner, enjoying the same hobbies, then they may react more sensitively to change at work in comparison with someone who regularly seeks out new jobs and has frequently changed organizations, locations and colleagues.

Another consideration when asking people to learn new things is the volume of change that you are asking them to assimilate at the same time. If people can accept that each change is a psychological experience involving a feeling of loss and fear followed by acceptance and incorporation of the change into what is already known, then it is easy to see that the more change you ask people to become involved in, the more of these different emotional states they will be experiencing simultaneously. They will need space to process all of this new information and one of the ways you can support them with this is to create 'islands of stability': be very clear about what is not changing so that there are still some areas of their job that they can see remaining the same and can perform automatically without having to think through every step that they carry out.

Loss of productivity

Unfortunately, once people start to participate in the change their negative feelings will not disappear immediately. As they start to figure out how to work differently, they have to try new things and do things for the first time. This can often create a sense of frustration and anger because the first few times we do things we make mistakes and go slower than normally.

If you think about the old ways of working, your team probably haven't made a mistake in a long time. When we make mistakes we feel stupid, we get annoyed with ourselves and others. We might feel that the situation is unfair. We used to be good at our job and now we are making the same mistakes as new joiners.

People have less confidence in the new task; they are not sure what all of the next steps are so they may have to refer to notes or ask someone to tell them what happens next. This means that work is completed more slowly and less work gets done. People may therefore feel that they have contributed less even though they may be putting in a huge amount of effort and probably feel quite tired; they are also worried that they should stay late and increase the amount they have accomplished for the day.

Mistakes and slow progress combine to make people feel angry about having to change and they will naturally want to return to the old ways of working. They might come up with lots of reasons why it would be better to abandon the change: they might compare it unfavourably with the old ways of working or they might find problems or errors that were not known at the start. Instead of overcoming these problems, some people will use them as a reason to stop the change.

Figure 6.4 Level of productivity during change

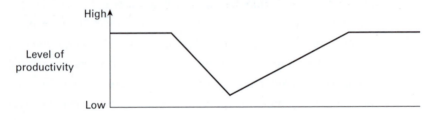

Appreciating the new state

If people stick with the change, and continue to try the new ways of working, it will become more familiar and automatic. They will make fewer mistakes and will be able to work at a faster rate. People will feel more confidence in their ability to work in the new way and they will start to forget how they used to work.

Once confidence begins to return, people start to enjoy themselves; they become more positive and this makes them more open to new ideas. So they review the new ways of working, see the advantages and look for ways to apply these advantages to other areas of their work. It is at this point that the change becomes embedded in how they do things and they are capable of realizing the benefits that were expected of it.

When you are leading change you have to recognize the impact that these five emotional states can have on people's productivity and try not to penalize people for lower performance levels as they strive to adapt to the new ways of working. Any negative comments made about productivity during this period can be particularly incendiary as your team are likely to be feeling under pressure because of the additional effort to learn new things. During the early stages of change, as people try to assimilate new ways of working, there is an unfortunate spike in activity coupled with a dip in productivity that generates stress and anxiety.

Figure 6.5 Activity versus productivity during change

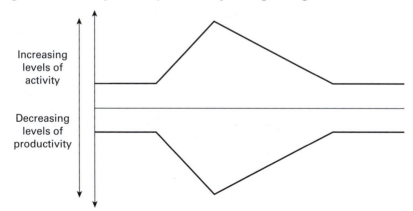

Increasing
levels of
activity

Decreasing
levels of
productivity

Environment needs to provide encouragement

The environment that you create when implementing the change must encourage all those impacted to take part by giving them the confidence to get started and to keep going when problems arise.

This confidence is generated by a positive environment that encourages people to view change as something enjoyable and meaningful. A positive environment encourages optimism over pessimism and emphasizes successes over failures. It is a simple concept, best described as looking for the good in every situation.

Optimism is the tendency to expect the best possible outcome and seek out the most hopeful aspects of a situation. Studies have shown that when we are feeling optimistic we are more able to identify positive aspects of a situation, which fuels our optimism so it becomes a virtuous circle (Figure 6.6), helping us to create a 'can do attitude' and a belief in our ability to be successful.

It is easier to feel positive about a change if it is set in the context of existing success. If the culture tends to emphasize the negative it is harder for people to justify the personal cost of putting additional effort into change. In an environment that emphasizes recent failures and current problems it is hard to envisage how this latest change could buck the trend and be successful. At an organizational level this involves emphasizing what is good today, how successful the organization already is, the advantages it enjoys over its competitors and the positive relationships that exist with customers, suppliers, regulators and other opinion formers. As change leaders you must

Figure 6.6 Virtuous circle of optimism

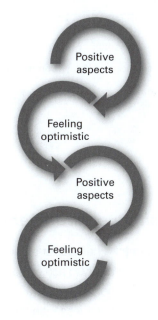

also emphasize how the organization has triumphed over adversity with examples of past problems and their solutions, and how these solutions are now generating benefits.

Another element of the positive environment is that there is a no blame culture. This means people feel able to report the truth rather than fabricate results that would look more impressive. Blame is a negative emotion which concentrates on what is wrong and who is responsible for the failure rather than seeking out what works, praising the progress so far and encouraging further achievement.

The positive environment you create has to have integrity. That means challenges cannot be ignored but they can be positively explained. For example, if there are more errors than expected found in the data which is due to be loaded into a new system, consider explaining the advantages of being able to fix these errors and start working with the new system with good quality data. This means you are recognizing the issue, but also finding a benefit to addressing it.

This links to what I mentioned in Chapter 5: Relationship building, regarding the importance of controlling your emotions when faced with errors and problems. It takes self-control to maintain a positive stance as your first reaction may be anger or disappointment with those who were responsible for the quality of the data.

Figure 6.7 Virtuous circle of positivity

Resilience   Commitment

Creativity

Benefits of a positive environment

In recent years there have been a number of studies about the importance of a positive environment on our ability to achieve our objectives. This understanding is called positive psychology and is a relatively new field of psychology, having been in existence for less than 30 years.

A positive environment creates a virtuous circle where the results of this positivity creates even greater levels of positivity, the results of which include commitment to our work, creativity in how we solve problems and resilience in the face of difficulties (Figure 6.7).

An important benefit of a positive environment is its ability to increase commitment to the task we are involved in. If people believe their environment to be safe and rewarding then they increase the amount of discretionary effort they are prepared to give to their work. Examples of this discretionary effort include volunteering for extra tasks, staying late to finish work or coming in early to give a task more of your time. Creating this willingness to put in extra effort is vital for the success of change initiatives. As change leaders you are unlikely to have hierarchical authority over those impacted by the change who need to alter the way they work to fit in with the new circumstances that you are creating. You are instead relying on this voluntary extra effort.

Studies have shown that a positive environment increases levels of creativity and problem solving. This is essential for change as so many issues will arise which have not been experienced before, and for which new solutions will need to be devised. A positive environment means people are:

- more creative, with the ability of greater lateral thinking which means they are more successful at problem solving;

- more open to new information, able to process it more effectively and able to consider more aspects of a situation simultaneously;

- able to show more generosity in their dealings with others, which reduces the level of conflict and means people have more energy to bring to their tasks.

Resilience and change

Resilience is the ability to control how to respond to situations and how we bounce back from adversity. Those with greater levels of commitment to their task are more willing to keep going even when things are not going well. Those with greater levels of creativity are more able to believe that they will overcome the adversity as they have greater levels of confidence in their ability to solve problems. These factors feed the level of resilience that someone has when faced with the fear and uncertainty that change in the workplace can generate.

As change leaders it's important to foster high levels of resilience. If those impacted by change have low levels of resilience then it reduces the number of people engaged with the change that have the willingness to work through the difficult times. This reduces the total amount of energy and enthusiasm, which can decrease the level of commitment, creativity and resilience of all. This lack of resilience can easily spiral into a negative environment where the failure of the change becomes a self-fulfilling prophecy.

Resilience is powered by the internal motivation for change (see pages 221–35) but as change leaders you can support its development by monitoring your changes for early signs of problems and providing support as soon as problems emerge, and before people become overwhelmed by them. You can also help by identifying examples of past problems and how they were overcome.

How to create a positive environment

Creating a positive environment takes a lot of effort, because humans have a bias towards negativity. From our earliest evolution our biology has encouraged us to assess our situation for danger so that we can respond to it quickly. Research in neuroscience has found that we maintain that bias today, so even though we are no longer cave dwellers always watchful for attacks by predators, we use the same type of thinking in every new situation we encounter.

This negative bias manifests itself in two ways: 1) we are naturally predisposed to identify what is wrong with a situation before we identify what is right with it; and 2) negative feelings are stronger and last in our brain longer. Positive feelings are more fleeting so they can only give us a temporary boost.

As a change leader you can overcome this bias by engaging with those impacted by the change in specific ways. The first is to ensure that whenever you are seeking out the opinion of those affected by change, you ask them to identify the benefits, improvements and helpful effects of the change. We should avoid asking them to identify what might go wrong with the change or how it might negatively impact them. We are not ignoring negative aspects of the change, we are just recognizing that we do not need to ask for this information as those involved will volunteer this information as it already dominates their thoughts, thanks to the negative bias.

Case example

Carol is an experienced director of transformational change programmes. She has over 20 years of corporate experience and works at very senior levels within her organization. She believes that one of the keys to her success is helping people find the good in the changes that she proposes. When she leads workshops to plan new ways of working, she runs sessions on identifying the context for change using the SWOT (strengths, weaknesses, opportunities and threats) technique. Carol has learnt that if she asks her groups to provide information on all four headings, then the workshop is likely to be critical of the change. However, if she asks her groups to identify information relevant to the strengths of the change and the opportunities that it will provide, then the atmosphere is more positive. She hears the participants talking about the threats and the weaknesses but she has not asked for this information so it is not emphasized when they feed back their views to her. In this way, Carol can ask people how they will participate in making the change a reality without giving them a platform for outlining why the change is a bad idea in the first place!

Creating a positive environment takes a lot of effort, so make it as easy as possible by minimizing the input of negative people and maximizing the contribution of those who are naturally positive personalities. For example, look to those who are more apt to look on the downside of life to contribute to the change by testing, quality reviewing and critiquing the work. Ask those who are naturally enthusiastic and engaged to take the lead in the communications activities that will have the greatest effect on the atmosphere and the attitude of others. As we shall see later in this chapter, by asking the optimists to use their core talents of looking for good news, and the pessimists to help increase the quality of our change outcomes, you can increase the level of participation in the creation of a positive environment.

Points to consider

Where can you source information about the past successes of your organization?

Review those impacted by your change and decide which of them are the strongest optimists and which of them are more naturally pessimistic.

Another facet of the negative bias that we must address is how negative thoughts have the strength to outweigh positive thoughts. For this reason, you need to surround every negative thought with a number of positive thoughts (Figure 6.8). There have been various studies assessing high performing teams which indicate that for every negative aspect of a change, it should be overwhelmed with at least three positive factors just to keep things in balance.

Figure 6.8 Overwhelming negative thoughts with positive thoughts

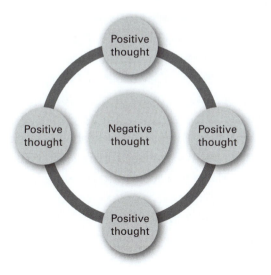

Every time someone is able to identify a positive aspect of the change you have the opportunity to push the negative aspects into the background. However, this is temporary so you need to keep the flow of positive thoughts continually flowing so that they keep pushing the negative to the backs of people's minds.

Case example

Sonia is responsible for a large team of change managers in a food manufacturer that produces pre-prepared meals for the airline industry. She feels that her workplace is strongly attuned to the negative bias, as every innovation is greeted with an extensive list of reasons why the production line cannot be changed, or why customers would not like a suggested new recipe. For this reason she has told her change managers that part of their role is to act as a mixture of journalist and advertising executive, seeking out and communicating positive news about the changes they are involved in. She has equated this to their own version of the production line, constantly churning out positive feelings about what they are trying to accomplish and delivering them regularly to all those impacted by their changes, before they have time to think up reasons why they should not change.

Techniques for positive thinking

It is vital to work collaboratively with your colleagues in order to establish this positive environment. Everyone will have a different view of what success looks like so the more people you ask, the more ideas you will get. Make sure that finding good things to say about the change is a regular agenda item for any workshops you run or any meetings that you chair.

If you want people to feel engaged with the change and to feel positive about its effects then they will need to be clear about what success looks like and have worked out the role that they can play in that success. You need them to be concerned for the outcome and emotionally committed to it, so the outcome has to contribute to a positive environment at work because that is what people will be drawn to.

One way you can help people to establish a positive frame of mind is to encourage them to identify three aspects of their work and their working environment that they are pleased with, grateful for or proud of. This might include:

- how people feel about their work and the actions that have led them to where they are today;
- knowledge or skills that they have acquired over their career;
- problems that they have solved for themselves or for others;
- places or people that they get to visit as part of their role;
- the relationship that they have with their colleagues;
- their physical working environment.

This exercise works well if it is enforced over a number of days, with individuals being asked to identify a different three things every day. It is an easy exercise to begin with, because you write down whatever makes you smile. As the days progress it becomes harder because you have to come up with something different every day and that makes you review what you have already written (which reinforces the positive aspects of your work) and think about more specific aspects of your work that you enjoy or get satisfaction from.

The benefits of this exercise are that it:

- Encourages you to scan for the positive aspects of a situation before looking at the negative.
- Enables you to re-live positive experiences as identifying them and writing them down is an opportunity to think them through and enjoy them all over again.
- Helps you see how problems have been solved in the past which reinforces your confidence in handling new challenges.
- Enables you to identify the strengths and skills that you already have, and improves your ability to volunteer for aspects of the change that fit with your core skills and talents. This helps to increase the level of intrinsic motivation that you have for seeing the change through to a successful conclusion.

> ## Case example
>
> Asad was involved in an organizational change that had a dramatic impact on his work including changes to location, who he worked with, his responsibilities and the skills he needed. His change manager introduced this technique at one of the early change management workshops and encouraged everyone impacted by the change to give it a try.
>
> When Asad tried the technique he found that initially he was identifying quite big items that were not very specific. For example, Asad wrote down that he was grateful for his easy journey to work and that he liked and enjoyed the company of his colleagues. As the days passed Asad found his comments were becoming much more specific and in the last week of the exercise he was identifying specific issues that he was pleased with. For example, he wrote about a meeting that he felt positive about, and how much he had enjoyed giving praise to one of his colleagues because he could see how much it reassured his colleague.
>
> Asad found that the more specific comments were very useful as things got tougher in his new job because it gave him real examples of where he was doing OK or had the knowledge to do the work which gave him the confidence to try other things. Although Asad does not write a list of positive items every day, he still uses this technique at the start of a difficult piece of work, to inspire himself to begin by reassuring himself he has achieved other difficult things in the past. This is helpful as things continue to change at work and he is under pressure to continue to develop his skills.

Different people will have different reasons for feeling positive about the change, depending on their personalities and relevant past experiences. The environment you create must allow for this range of expression, as long as the underlying theme is positive. For example:

- Some people will be encouraged by the opportunities presented by a bright new future, described in terms of what can be achieved and what the benefits of these achievements are without reference to the situation that exists today.

- Others are encouraged by the idea of how the problems that they have today will be resolved by the new future resulting from the change. They will want to list each of these improvements with careful reference to the current situation.

- Some people will be encouraged by defining in detail exactly how things will work in the future whilst others prefer to concentrate on a broad outline.

- Others will seek evidence that this type of future state has already been successfully achieved elsewhere whilst some are happy to enter the unknown.

Building a sustaining environment

As an effective change leader it is important to create an environment that is able to sustain the effort required to make change a reality, not just at the beginning when things feel exciting or at the end when there is a sense of satisfaction.

When change begins to be implemented, levels of confidence and motivation can fall and levels of anxiety and stress can rise. This is because:

- the extra effort needed to work in new ways whilst forgetting how to work in the old way is significant;

- mistakes are made and although they should be expected, they can cause worry and they can take time to fix so productivity will fall;

- things don't go smoothly and inevitably progress and achievements deviate from the plan, sometimes necessitating re-planning and/or reworking what has already been implemented to respond to negative feedback.

The environment needs to encourage continuation with the change, emphasizing the need to keep going, even though it feels difficult. It is at this point that many involved in change want to reduce the level of energy that they are applying. This lack of energy decreases the effort that they make, which reduces the number of successes that they have, which in turn feeds their boredom with the change activities, leading to a lack of energy being applied.

For this reason the environment needs to encourage and acknowledge perseverance. Perseverance comes from motivation to change (see pages 221–35) and the physical energy to carry out the work.

It is your responsibility to assess the energy levels of those involved in the change and manage their contribution so that everyone is able to balance time when less effort is made, so that individuals are able to recharge and replenish their enthusiasm for making improvements and learning new skills, and time when heightened energy is applied during critical parts of the change lifecycle, eg the early days of deployment.

Tracking energy levels

Although organizations are faced with a continual cycle of change, people cannot maintain maximum levels of participation in every change all of the time. If you expect those impacted to operate at their peak continually they will become exhausted, make mistakes and lose their motivation for change. This will lead them to withdraw their discretionary effort.

As change leaders you need to identify when these peaks of energy will be required so that you can smooth the change plan to balance times of critical effort with periods of rest and recharging. This means identifying some periods when the proportion of work that an individual regards as stable is higher than the proportion of work that is subject to change. Effectively you are creating 'islands of stability'. This stability comes from undertaking work that an individual has built up a level of competency in, so that they are able to carry out the work without having to consult user guides or ask their colleagues what they should do next after every step. Aspects of the work that remain unchanged offer 'islands of stability' that are restful to carry out in comparison with the activities that have been changed because individuals have unconscious competence that allows them to carry out the work automatically, with normal levels of performance.

You can create this stability by managing the scope of your change to ensure that some aspects of your existing working practices are retained. This conserves energy because not everything needs to be relearned. It also maintains a level of confidence, as individuals are not constantly practising new skills, which reassures them that they haven't lost all of their skills and knowledge and gives them a break between the periods of intense concentration needed for the things that are changing.

Another technique for preserving the energy for change is to balance the load of change that is happening at any one time. Productivity falls during the transition to new ways of working, but this period of lower productivity can be extended considerably if further changes are added before the initial changes have been embedded.

In Figure 6.9 we can see that the original planned change led to a fall of productivity to position 1. However, before productivity could return to normal levels, another change was implemented which further depressed productivity levels to position 2 and a subsequent change depressed productivity even further to position 3. Those impacted by these changes are in danger of suffering from 'change fatigue' as they have had to assimilate three changes

Figure 6.9 Impact of continuous change

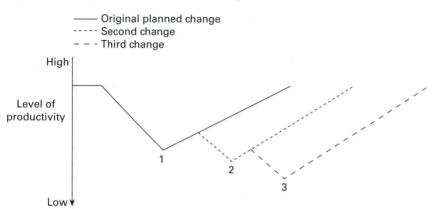

in swift succession, and the time at which they will return to normal levels of productivity keeps being pushed out of reach.

To ensure continued change does not reduce the commitment to change, consider agreeing a productivity level which must be reached before subsequent changes can be implemented. Alternatively, agree a period of time when lower productivity will be accepted, and do not initiate any more change until work has returned to normal and staff are able to recharge their energy levels in preparation for the next round of changes.

Case example

Lawrence works in a test laboratory that tests the properties of different plastics for industry. As a change leader, he believes that the most important thing is to be upfront about the impact of change on productivity, so that the expectations of staff and customers can be managed. He believes that a lot of change initiatives put themselves under pressure because they convince themselves that because the change is positive, there will be no impact on productivity. His experience proves otherwise. Lawrence says it doesn't matter whether you train in advance of going live or you train people in the new ways of working once the new equipment has become available – people will still need time and energy to work out how to do their job in the new way, and this period of adjustment must be factored into your change plan to prevent destabilization of the business as usual environment. When Lawrence implements changes to the equipment used in the lab or changes the processes that are used for testing, he balances the expected falls in productivity with times in the lab when there is less demand for their services.

Predicting energy levels

When energy levels are falling, it is helpful to diagnose what is causing the problem so that the response you suggest is appropriate. For example, energy can become low when the change leader only hears feedback or comparison from their own team who are struggling to make the change a success. Their comments are focused on their experience and their difficulties and are likely to be expressions of anger, confusion or exhaustion, especially as they grapple with the changes in the early stages.

If you think those involved in the change are being worn down by this then identify other sources of feedback outside of their direct team that could give them a different perspective. Consider talking to others in the organization that have already adopted these changes and are now feeling more positive about them. Or review the community map (stakeholder analysis) and find customers, suppliers, regulators, different functions etc who are in favour of the changes and will encourage those involved to keep going.

If a lot of work has been done but everyone is aware there is a still a lot more to do then consider consolidating what has been done. Call a halt to further adoption and bring people together to map where they started from and each step that they have successfully achieved. From this they can start to see how far they have come, and can take pride in their achievements. This generates a positive belief in their ability to keep going and can help them more accurately predict the remaining effort required, which may not be as much as they think.

If there is paralysis of action because the next steps feel so big it is difficult to know where to get started. In this case it's important to spend time on breaking down these tasks into their sub-tasks, and each sub-task into further sub-tasks. From this more micro approach it is easier to understand which tasks should come first, and which should come next. Also, by breaking the work down into much smaller pieces, it is easier to get started because you are only committing to a small piece of work at a time which feels less daunting.

Points to consider

How do you balance your energy levels so that you do not become overwhelmed?

How can you apply these ideas to those impacted by your change?

Environment needs to provide motivation

What is motivation?

Motivation is derived from the Latin word *movere*, which means to move. If we are motivated then we are moved or driven to do something. Motivation is psychological; it is an internal force that leads us to take certain decisions.

We will decide to contribute effort to a task based on our assessment of the importance of the task, the value of the task and the consequences of not doing it. This assessment gives us our inner drive to do something and the importance we attach to the task will determine the level of drive or commitment that we have. Would you spend your weekend on a work-related task unless you had decided that it was important? You are unlikely to give up your free time unless you have assessed the situation and decided that there is greater value in completing the task than in having free time.

This personal assessment of the situation that we undertake is affected by external factors or internal values and beliefs. If we are motivated by external factors then we are experiencing extrinsic motivation. Extrinsic motivation comes from outside factors, which can be summarized as rewards or threats. We may decide to commit to a task because the rewards are attractive and will give us pleasure. For example, a pay rise, promotion, award or recognition from our colleagues or the wider marketplace can be strong motivating factors. Threats or punishments can also be powerful motivating factors. For example, exclusion from a bonus scheme or the removal of responsibilities and status from our jobs can drive us to participate in specific activities.

When you seek to generate participation in change activities, and motivate people to create and adopt new ways of working, extrinsic motivation has several limitations. First, being driven by external factors means that an individual can feel coerced into carrying out the task, particularly if their decision was based on threats and punishments. An individual may be contributing to the task but they may harbour resentment and resistance or disinterest. This can impact the rate and the quality of their work, and will require management oversight to ensure completion meets requirements. Second, change is a collaborative effort which requires everyone whose responsibilities are affected to make changes to their ways of working. Those of us leading the change effort are often colleagues of those involved and as such we do not have any authority over them. Even if you are in a line management position, you are unlikely to have the authority to award bonuses or pay rises or exclude staff from rewards packages or demote them.

Intrinsic motivation

To successfully implement change you need to rely on intrinsic motivation. This type of motivation comes from within and is based on personal values and beliefs. If you are intrinsically motivated you have decided to participate in something because of its inherent interest or attractiveness.

Accessing the intrinsic motivation of those involved in the change has several advantages:

1 Numerous studies have concluded that those motivated intrinsically are more likely to engage in the task willingly, and demonstrate higher levels of creativity and willingness to learn and develop their skills during the task.

2 Intrinsic motivation does not cost the organization anything. It does not rely on additional rewards and it does not expose the organization to the risks of inadequately thought through punishments including claims for compensation and unfair dismissal.

3 The use of intrinsic motivation aligns to the desire of staff to take more responsibility for their own work. Increasingly organizations are shifting from the 'command and control structure' model to flat hierarchies and matrix management where knowledge and ability determine power rather than job title and length of service.

Generating a flow

Intrinsic motivation is linked by some to our level of spiritual intelligence. Spiritual intelligence is a phrase used by some psychologists and philosophers to define an additional intelligence to analytical intelligence (often referred to as IQ) and emotional intelligence (EQ). Spiritual intelligence is an awareness of our meaning, value and contribution in the world. Those with spiritual intelligence are able to stand back from situations and appreciate their wider context, and to demonstrate high levels of empathy with others. They are very aware of what motivates them and why they behave the way that they do and they are comfortable with these answers. Intrinsic motivation is a powerful force because it is linked to our need to add value and make a substantive contribution as a result of our work.

Figure 6.10 Factors that lead to flow

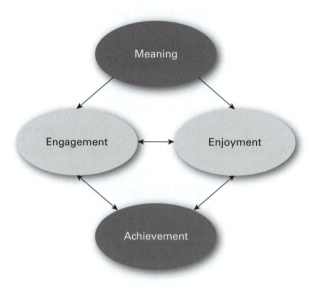

Intrinsic motivation can generate flow or mindfulness in those undertaking their tasks. These are popular terms to describe a state of total immersion or concentration. When we are experiencing flow we focus on a task to the exclusion of all other work and we become so involved in what we are doing we stop noticing the amount of time we are spending on it. We are also more able to ignore interruptions from others and from ourselves in that we tend not to multi-task or become distracted by other activities.

Flow begins with meaning. In order to become immersed in an activity, the activity has to achieve one of our objectives or be important in the context of what we are doing. This meaning is personal to us and might include a belief that we are doing important work, or the task gives us an opportunity to learn something new or work with people whose company we enjoy. This meaning drives our ability to engage with and enjoy the task. In Figure 6.10 there are double-headed arrows between engagement, enjoyment and achievement because absorption in the task is enjoyable, and enjoyment increases our engagement with the task.

Managing flow

Achieving this flow leads to a significant increase in our productivity and is becoming an important consideration when designing work, as the productivity improvements are an important efficiency benefit. Numerous studies have measured the effect of interruptions on our rate and quality of work and found that on average nearly half of those working in offices only get 15 minutes before they are interrupted, and that at least an hour a day is wasted dealing with these distractions, including the time lost gathering our thoughts and re-focusing on the task. Importantly, these studies point out that interruptions prevent people from reaching a state where they can think creatively and innovate, which are essential elements of defining new ways of working.

Another aspect of achieving flow is to ensure that the difficulty of the task is matched with your skill. Factors that encourage flow include being clear about what you are trying to achieve and getting feedback as you are doing the task that you are doing a good job. So it needs to be a task where you can see you are making progress, which builds your confidence that you are doing well which gives you the encouragement to continue with it.

Factors that impact your ability to achieve flow include concerns about failing and interruptions that break your concentration. If you are under pressure to deliver a piece of work to a certain standard or by a specific deadline then it will be harder to lose yourself in the creative process. Your train of thought and your ability to focus on the task will be affected by other demands for your attention so work somewhere that phones, e-mails and other people can't interrupt you.

Points to consider

When was the last time you became completely absorbed in a work task that you didn't notice the passing of time?

What factors contributed to this situation?

How can you create similar conditions for those impacted by your change?

Creating intrinsic motivation

As shown in Figure 6.11 intrinsic motivation is a product of a number of factors:

- Meaningfulness – belief in the importance of the change within the organization and within the market in which the organization operates. Meaningfulness results from a positive assessment of the validity of the change and a conclusion that it is logical and sensible.

Figure 6.11 Creation of intrinsic motivation

Figure 6.12 Intrinsic motivation develops energy and enjoyment

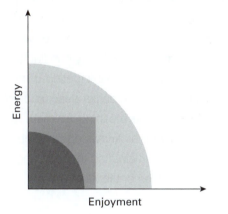

- Autonomy – the power of the individual to make their own decisions and have control over their work.

- Talents – the opportunity for individuals to use their core strengths and abilities in their work.

These factors combine to create a level of enthusiasm and interest in the change activities, and this enthusiasm forms part of our intrinsic motivation, which drives our participation in the change, as shown in Figure 6.12.

Meaningfulness

Meaningfulness is an important element of motivation. Everyone has to find their own reason for participating in the change. Sometimes there is an obvious benefit and the person is one of the winners. For example, if a process for entering customer information is automated then the person responsible for the data no longer has to enter it manually. This reduces errors and decreases the number of corrections they have to make, which increases their enjoyment of their work.

In other cases, individuals will need to be given time to think through the implications of the change before they are able to discover any improvements or benefits that are personal to them. These benefits may not be apparent to others but that is fine. As long as they mean something to that individual the benefits will act as a motivating force. For example, there may be aspects of their job that they find tedious and dislike doing which may now be removed. Some people might see this as a loss of power but the affected individual is happy to lose work that they never enjoyed in the first place.

Finally, there will always be some individuals for whom the change has little meaning. They may regard the new ways of working as 'more of the same'. You might be wondering where they can find the meaning and what the personal reasons might be for participating in the change. For these people we have to think back to the earlier description of how change feels. The change itself may have little meaning for them, but being part of the team and being respected for their knowledge and ability does have significant value. Their reason for participating in the change is to remain part of the group and make a valuable contribution.

Autonomy

Autonomy is a very important factor in generating participation in the change. Empowering individuals to decide for themselves how they will become involved in the change increases their desire to participate and commit to the activities. When someone chooses to do something for themselves they are naturally more interested in it, and more likely to see it through to completion. People need to convince themselves that they have made the right decision and will put effort into making that a self-fulfilling prophecy.

Autonomy is not just about deciding what change activities to become involved in. You also need to create an environment that supports individual decision making about the change as a whole and the amount of power that we are prepared to transfer to others.

Indicators of autonomy in our working environment include:

- allowing individuals to select the tasks for which they feel most skilled and able;
- allowing individuals to decide how a task is to be completed including the techniques they will use and the resources they require;
- consulting with individuals so that they can provide ideas and feedback and see that their contribution is fairly evaluated and actioned where appropriate;

- including individuals in the governance and decision making processes for the change;
- challenging individuals to solve problems and take responsibility for implementing the solutions for these problems;
- balancing the level of responsibility given to individuals with the level of guidance and support that is offered, so that autonomy does not become abandonment.

Talents

I have used the word 'talents' to describe core skills, natural abilities and preferences for the types of things we like to do. This is because there is a strong link between what we like to do and what we are good at doing.

As shown in Figure 6.13, people find tasks that require using their skills and talents infinitely more easy. These skills may come naturally or are the product of past experience and practice, nevertheless because they find something easy to do, they volunteer to do more of it; as they do more of it they become even better at it which makes it even easier to do. The easier the task is the more enjoyment we get from doing it. This links to intrinsic motivation in that we are attracted to the task so we are willing to commit time and effort to it.

Figure 6.13 Task preference/task competence cycle

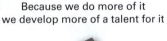

Because it is easy to do
we volunteer to do more of it

Because we do more of it
we develop more of a talent for it

Easy because we are
using our natural talents

Task is easy to do

The easiest way to achieve this virtuous circle is to encourage people to play to their strengths and talents which naturally generates engagement and therefore participation in the change which drives performance.

To demonstrate this model for yourself, think about your job and identify your favourite task or piece of work. Think about how you approach the work, what you like to do first, what you do next. Consider if you do it with other people or whether you work alone. Imagine yourself carrying out this activity. Can you picture yourself enjoying the work? Are you feeling satisfied in your ability to complete it successfully? Are you smiling? Yes, you probably are.

For a different approach, imagine having to do something that you really dislike. Imagine yourself carrying it out. Do you feel angry or resentful? Do you feel relieved when it is finished? Are you smiling? No, probably not.

An advantage of this approach is that enjoyment of the task can help to override resistance to change. As we saw earlier in this chapter, part of people's natural resistance to change is fear that they will not be able to cope with the new ways of working. This fear dissipates as they contribute to the change by using their existing skills. Whilst people will still have to learn new things, they have less anxiety because by doing things they are good at they are able to reinforce a positive view of their abilities, which boosts confidence. In some cases, the opportunities to do things that individuals like doing can override their resistance to changes that they do not believe are valid or worthwhile. Using our natural talents gives us pleasure and people are willing to participate in the change to access this pleasure, even though they would prefer the change not to be taking place at all.

Applying existing skills and talents is a pragmatic approach because it is time effective. Asking people to carry out tasks that do not use their skills means they go more slowly than others who have a natural aptitude for the work. Overcoming weaknesses is time consuming and is pushing against the prevailing tide. If someone was going to be any good at something they probably would have acquired these skills by now.

Using an agile approach, the priority is to implement the change as quickly as possible and clear the path for the next change and the one after that. So it is not the best use of time to go off and invest in personal development activities and performance management to help someone understand what they are getting wrong and showing them how they could improve.

Different preferences

To enable people to apply their talents to the change initiative, we first have to consider the different types of skills that they have. There are lots of models that help us understand our skills, competencies and preferences, but to keep things simple I have summarized three different groups of preferences.

Focused on the task, getting things done and organizing the work People in this group will seek out activities that enable them to:

- create a plan or a to do list;
- create ways to track and report on progress;
- break the activity into individual steps and organize them into a priority order;
- look ahead for things that could prevent progress on the task;
- re-arrange the work in response to changes in the situation.

Value of the task and the contribution that it makes People in this group will seek out activities that enable them to:

- find sources of information about the task;
- review the details including contracts, financial records, performance metrics;
- analyse information about the task;
- set the change in the wider context;
- set discipline or controls for the task.

Relationships and bringing people together People in this group will seek out activities that enable them to:

- explain the task to others;
- make sure everyone has a role and is involved in the change;
- network and bring people together to form new relationships;
- give people an opportunity to develop their skills;
- encourage people to voice their opinions.

How do you know who has which talents?

The obvious answer is to ask people to volunteer for their work or offer their services. Their natural inclination will be to volunteer for the tasks that they would most enjoy doing.

Encourage people to think outside of their job title or job description and identify things that they do outside of work that is not part of their existing role. Numerous lifestyle surveys conclude that most of us employ talents and skills outside of the workplace that we never employ at work.

This is a waste because we put more effort into what we enjoy. We work through lunch, come in early or stay late, power through the boring stuff to create time to do what we enjoy. We do more research and teach ourselves more about subjects we like. We study for additional qualifications or net-work with others who share our interests. All of this builds our capability and creates additional capability for our organizations.

Break the change into its required talents

To do this:

- find people's talents – take your change and work with people to identify what skills, strengths and talents they believe will be associated with making it a success;

- either work through the change using an end-to-end process model like SIPOC or look at the change from all of its constituent parts, eg product breakdown structure, architecture map etc;

- then you need to get those involved to break the change down further into the required activities and then look at the activities against the required talents.

This is important because even though you want individuals in your team to self-nominate you still need to ensure that all of the tasks, even the boring ones, are undertaken – the advantage of this approach is that something one person might regard as boring will tap into someone else's talent and preferred way of working.

Points to consider

Think about the change that you are involved in. What type of skills and abilities are critical to success?

Are these skills commonly associated with the work that your organization does, or will new skills need to be developed?

Example of intrinsic motivation

To demonstrate the enthusiasm that utilizing intrinsic motivation can provide, let's work through an example.

In addition to your normal work, you and several colleagues have been asked to organize a one-day conference on the latest developments in your field of expertise. You will need to arrange for speakers from your organization and from other bodies including universities and professional associations to contribute and you will need to arrange for an external venue. You have been asked to invite customers and potential customers as well as senior managers from within your organization.

In an initial meeting with your colleagues you have identified the following streams of work:

- venue and catering;
- speakers and agenda;
- invitations and publicity.

There is a lot of energy in the room as you and your colleagues start to identify what needs to be done and who is going to do it. Although you are all focused on the same task you are each pursuing your own approach to the work.

One of your colleagues (Shana) is quietly working away at the back of the room, writing sticky notes for each activity and putting them on a flipchart. She has drawn a chart of activity, time and person responsible and is endeavouring to fill this in. Shana is asking lots of questions about conferences that the organization has run before, trying to identify things that might cause problems and how these might be overcome. She is asking the rest of you if you have any experience in insuring these types of events. She has proposed a template for progress reporting and is suggesting weekly team meetings to discuss actions and issues.

Another colleague (Nick) is thinking aloud about how the conference might be perceived in the marketplace and how customers and competitors might react. He is interested in the background to the event and is wondering why senior management have decided to go ahead when a similar event was postponed six months ago. He has started to identify potential benefits that can be realized from the event and which areas of the business are going to be most positively impacted. He has turned to Shana, who is creating the to-do list and suggested that the contracts team will need to be involved in creating contracts with the venue and the caterers, and that it would be sensible to define success criteria for the venue so that a desk review can be done on possible locations before spending time visiting them.

A third colleague (Jan) is considering the relationships that the organization already has with professional bodies and universities and how inviting other universities might affect existing relationships. She is interested to find out which senior managers are the best public speakers and which of them have existing relationships with the universities and professional associations. She is also considering which senior managers get on best with each other and has identified some clashes of personality that will need to be considered when creating the seating plan. Hearing about the success criteria for the venue, she has volunteered to work with the PR department of the hotel or conference centre to try and get media coverage.

Each of these people are using their own talents and skills. They are motivated because they have been allowed to start work on the activities that naturally interest or excite them and they are enjoying the work. They are freely contributing their ideas and are showing commitment to doing an excellent job and participating fully in the event.

Now imagine a different situation. Instead of allowing a free flow of ideas and self-selection about the work involved, the tasks have been allocated to each of your colleagues.

Shana has been asked to undertake a cost benefit analysis, identifying how the event aligns to the strategic objectives of the organization, defining which departments are likely to gain the most from the event and to provide a full breakdown of all the costs.

Nick has been asked to review all attendance from inside the organization and how each member of your organization can be matched with a speaker from a university or professional association.

Jan has been asked to create a project plan and reporting mechanism to manage the event from today until successful completion.

All of your colleagues are capable of completing the tasks assigned to them, but they have had no say in how the work was allocated or why they were chosen for the tasks. This lack of autonomy dampens their enthusiasm because they do not feel they have control over their work or the freedom to do it how they think it should be done.

As the tasks run counter to their natural preferences they will schedule to complete them, but they are not becoming immediately involved. They will do the work but it might not get to the top of their priority list and they are likely to come up with other things to do ahead of completing these tasks. This could mean that their work is rushed and is not done to the same level of quality as someone with a genuine interest in it.

Applying motivation to clear goals

It is important to establish intrinsic motivation but at the same time this motivation must not be uncontrolled. It is important that all those involved in the change effort set well-formed goals that meet their personal ambitions and the needs of the team in achieving the change.

One model we can use for creating a well-formed goal is SMART:

- Specific – it needs to describe exactly how the skills and talents of the individual will be applied to help the change become a reality.

- Measurable – so that the person can track their progress and know when they are done.

- Attainable – there is no point setting a goal that is so ambitious it is unachievable as this will be demotivating.

- Realistic – based on your skills and your past experience, assess if what you are planning is realistic. Also consider the impact of other factors on your ability to get the work done, including the claims made on your time by your business as usual responsibilities.

- Timely – set a timeframe that is achievable but also fits with the work of others in the change team. The timeframe for achieving your goal links to its achievability because if the timeframe is too short the goal will be no longer be achievable.

An example format for a well formed goal is 'I will ... by X date, and my achievement will be evidenced by....'

For a recent change that I was involved in, I used my core talents for contingency planning and risk analysis (gained when I was the director of disaster recovery for a global organization) to define a clear goal:

> 'I will establish data recovery procedures for each of the offices across Europe by the end of March, and will test these plans individually and as an integrated response to a breach of data security.'

The description of the work is specific, and is relevant to my skill set. I know it is achievable because I have done it numerous times before and although I could get the work done earlier, the timeframe is realistic based on the other demands on my time. The timeframe also takes account of the need to wait for the work of other members of the change team to be completed, as their work is an input to mine.

Using the concept of intrinsic motivation to help identify who will undertake which tasks on your change plan can feel risky. One of the most common concerns is that individuals will select the most enjoyable tasks and leave the difficult activities to others. As the leader of your change, you have to take a practical stance. Begin by identifying at the higher level what types of change activities need to be undertaken and for which functions and departments they are required (shown in Table 6.1). In every meeting and discussion that you attend, add to the detail of this initial matrix (shown in Table 6.2).

Encourage people to help break these activities into more detail and to identify which aspects of the work they think they are best suited for. Once you have a proportion of the activities allocated to individuals through this voluntary method, review the outstanding tasks and go back to your resource pool to ask them to select additional work that has not yet been resourced.

Table 6.1 High level matrix of change activities

	Dept 1	Dept 2	Dept 3
Re-design processes			
Create new quality criteria			
Enter data into new systems			

This may sound time consuming, and certainly delegation of work by the change leader to the change team members is the quicker approach. However, once the change gets underway it becomes clear it is the slower approach; you will need to chase people to start work on things which they are not motivated to do, and you will need to closely track their efforts and encourage them to get involved, which you don't need to do if those you are working with are intrinsically motivated to participate in the change.

Table 6.2 Increased detail on matrix of change activities

	Dept 1		Dept 2			Dept 3	
	Team A	Team B	Team A	Team B	Team C	Team A	Team B
Re-design processes							
Customer contact processes							
Data quality processes							
Create new quality criteria							
Financial reporting							
Production levels							
Enter data into new systems							
Customer database							
Supplier database							

Conclusion

Your ability to persuade people to participate in the change is directly affected by the conditions that we create within which change takes place. Effective change leaders establish an environment that provides reassurance that the challenges associated with change have been recognized and that steps have been taken to ensure that those impacted will be encouraged, reassured and motivated throughout the lifecycle of the change.

Appendix 1
Change roles

Change sponsor

The person performing this role:

- has the authority necessary to implement the change across all areas impacted by the agreed scope;
- is personally committed to ensuring the change is a success;
- has strong relationships and a high level of credibility with all those impacted by the change.

Their responsibilities include:

1 working with all those impacted to create a description of the change that meets the business need and is regarded as feasible, appropriate and relevant to the challenges the organization faces;

2 establishing and maintaining alignment between the change and the organization's strategic objectives;

3 maintaining a balance between changing the business environment and achieving necessary performance levels;

4 championing the change by providing visible support within the organization and to all external parties with an interest in it;

5 willingly and proactively providing support and guidance to all those involved in making the change a reality;

6 demonstrating leadership of the change by modelling the behaviours expected as part of the new ways of working;

7 gaining access to and committing the necessary resources to the change;

8 devising and applying suitable governance arrangements that reflect the scale and risk associated with the change;

9 actively using the measures of the benefits to demonstrate what has been achieved, congratulating those responsible to generate support for and participation in the change;

10 actively using progress information and reviews to assess the progress of the change and take timely remedial action when necessary.

Points to consider when accepting this role:

- Do you have a clear understanding of how the organization will be different once the change has been implemented?

- Are you comfortable with your level of specialist knowledge in order to guide the overall direction of the change?

- Do you believe that the change is positive and has the capability to deliver sufficient business value to justify the investment in the change initiative?

- Do you have sufficient influence to effect change across all of the departments and functions involved?

- Can you commit sufficient time to take an active role as the sponsor and champion of this change?

Change leader

The person performing this role:

- is personally committed to ensuring the change is a success;

- has strong relationships and a high level of credibility with all those impacted by the change.

Their responsibilities include:

1 using specialist knowledge to contribute to the definition of business need and the description of the change that will meet this need;

2 comparing change activities against the organization's strategic objectives to prioritize the work to deliver the greatest business value;

3 committing the time and energy needed to repeatedly explain the scope, impact and benefits of the change to all those involved, and where relevant incorporating their feedback into the change activities;

4 willingly and proactively providing support and guidance to all those involved in making the change a reality;

5 demonstrating leadership of the change by modelling the behaviours expected as part of the new ways of working;

6 applying the governance arrangements and developing effective working relationships with the change sponsor and others in decision-making roles;

7 identifying and applying measures that prove that the change has realized benefits;

8 coordinating all of the change activities from all of the participants to create a comprehensive picture of progress, issues and risks;

9 escalating issues to the appropriate person and working with them to ensure they are resolved.

Points to consider when accepting this role:

- Do you have sufficient specialist knowledge of your organization, the market it operates within and the processes and systems impacted by the change to define the change activities?

- Has sufficient authority been delegated to enable you to coordinate the change across all of those impacted by it?

- Can you create sufficient time to perform your coordination of the change alongside your business as usual responsibilities?

Change participant

The person performing this role:

- actively participates in making changes to their way of working and contributes to changes in how others work;
- commits to the change activities voluntarily, using their own motivation to spur them into action, not relying on others to direct their contribution.

Their responsibilities include:

1 identifying how the business need that the change must deliver relates to their role and areas of responsibility;

2 clarifying the improvements that will be generated by the change and representing the change positively to all those impacted by it;

3 devising new ways of working to achieve the business need and realize the expected benefits;

4 collaborating with colleagues to identify and implement all necessary change activities;

5 participating in measuring the results of change to prove that benefits have been realized;

6 escalating issues to the appropriate person and working with them to ensure they are resolved.

Points to consider when accepting this role:

- Have you identified how you will benefit from making the change, and do you believe that they are necessary and an appropriate response?
- Are you clear about where you can add value and can you clearly articulate your contribution to the change effort?
- Can you create sufficient time to participate in the change alongside your business as usual responsibilities?

Appendix 2
Change management documents

This appendix describes the content of the documents created in Iteration 1 of the roadmap. I have kept the names of these documents as generic as possible as I recognize that you will rename them to fit with the prevailing terminology used in your own organization.

Description of the change

The purpose of the description of the change is to create an understanding of what will be different in the future. It is reviewed at the start of each iteration and acts as an important source of reference for what is required; helping to prioritize the work based on the intended scope and expected deliverables of the change. It contains the following elements:

Vision

There are three elements to the vision for your change:

1 description of the business environment once the change has been implemented, explaining the market position of your organization and its internal capabilities;

2 description of the transition state explaining how the new ways of working are balanced alongside some of the old practices that have not yet ended;

3 description of the environment during the change to reassure all those impacted that their contribution will be welcomed and that they will be offered support to help them adapt to the new business environment.

Too often, only the description of the business environment once the change has been implemented is provided. In order to build the confidence of those taking part in the change it is helpful to describe how work is prioritized and resourced during the transition state, so that individuals can define their role during the change.

The transition state is what those reading the description of the change will be operating within throughout the duration of the change initiative, so it is this that they will want to understand. The vision of the end state can offer an attractive future which is motivating, but this motivation will be outweighed by their concerns if they don't understand the structure of the transition state and level of support they will be given during transition.

Scope and exclusions

This is based on your interpretation of the business need and defines which areas of the business will be included in the change. These areas of the business can be a list of all of the departments or functions or might be listed by process, product or service. Some of the areas of the business included in the scope are not primary sources of the change but have to be included because they are the recipients of changes that they must accommodate by changing themselves. It is helpful to point out where these relationships exist to give those impacted confidence that the initial and subsequent effects of the change have been considered.

For completeness, this section should also define which areas are excluded from the change, with an explanation of why they have been excluded. It is important to balance the breadth of the impact of the change with the capability of the organization to cope with high levels of change, whilst at the same time maintaining acceptable levels of performance in the business as usual environment. For this reason, some areas may be excluded from the scope of the change initially, with the expectation that the changes will be rolled out to them at a later date.

Expected deliverables

Although the change will evolve as the results of each iteration triggers further ideas, and reactions to the change generate new requirements, there must be some agreement on the critical areas that will be subject to change: structural changes – processes, systems, buildings, roles and responsibilities – and cultural changes – behaviours, attitudes, skills and competences.

Assumptions

The vision, scope and deliverables have been defined as a result of an information-gathering exercise that analysed the business need and identified the benefits that meeting this business need would achieve. A number of assumptions will have already been made about your change initiative during this activity and they will need to be captured so that they are clear to everyone. It is also helpful to review them throughout the change because if these assumptions are no longer true then there may be an impact on what the change needs to achieve.

These assumptions will include prevailing beliefs in the internal capability of the organization, and the perception that customers, potential customers, suppliers, competitors and regulators have about the organization.

Constraints

Constraints are restrictions that the change will have to work around. In most change initiatives the biggest constraint is the availability of resources with sufficient experience of the current ways of working to help define new approaches, or with sufficient time to become involved in change as well as maintaining acceptable levels of productivity in their current role.

Links with other work

Interdependencies between this change initiative and other work planned or already underway might be regarded as a constraint but I have listed it separately as it may offer opportunities to benefit from work already done or to transfer some of the work to other teams working on similar changes.

In some organizations this description of the change will be created as a target operating model or blueprint of the future structure and capability of the organization. The danger with this approach is that this comprehensive definition of the future makes no allowances for responding to the real experience of change, where knowledge and experience develop incrementally as the impact of individual changes alter the perception of what else needs to change. For this reason I believe the description should be created as a series of ever more detailed documents, refined by those closest to the implementation of the change and revised at the end of every iteration.

The acceptance criteria for an effective description of the change are:

- it creates a positive description of the new working environment that reassures those that read it that the changes create genuine improvements in the internal capabilities and market position and reputation of the organization;

- it provides enough description of the change that individuals can understand how they will be impacted;

- there is an explanation of how the scope and deliverables align to the strategic objectives of the organization.

Business case

The purpose of the business case is to demonstrate why the change is needed and how it will deliver improvements to market position and internal capability over and above what exists today. In common with the change description, it is reviewed at the start of each iteration to understand what benefits the iteration should deliver, which in turn affects decisions on the priority of change ideas.

Throughout this book I have assumed that your job is to make change a reality, and not to decide if the organization should commit to the change. Therefore, I do not assume that you will be responsible for the creation of the business case, but I have included it here for the sake of completeness.

The most important information you will require will be a detailed under-standing of the benefits expected by the change, and you might find it more useful to have a detailed description of each benefit, which is not normally included within the business case. Therefore, at the end of this section I have set out what I would expect to see in a benefits description.

The business case often triggers the creation of a risk register, using the summary of risks from the business case as the initial entries in the risk register. If there is no business case for your change initiative or you do not have access to it, ensure that you create a register of all the risks to your successful implementation of the change.

The business case contains the following elements:

Benefits

The description of the benefits is derived from the business need that the change is addressing. The amount of detail that you include in your description of each benefit will be driven by the approach to benefits management that is used in your organization. As a minimum include the following:

- Type of benefit:
  - The most common type of benefit (and often the most popular as it is so easy to understand) is a financial benefit that summarizes the cost savings or the expected increases in revenue that will be created as a result of the change. Financial benefits also include a measure of profitability for each product or service.
  - Another type of benefit is often called a strategic benefit, which describes the improvement to the business resulting from the change. Strategic benefits include increases in the number or types of customers and the longevity of customer relationships.
  - Organizational benefits measure internal statistics including staff sickness, turnover, productivity per employee.
- Where in the organization the benefit will occur – as so much of our work is interconnected it is often very difficult (and not the most productive use of time) to narrow down one department or function that can claim the benefit as their own. Doing this does reduce the risks of double counting and overestimating the positive contribution of the change but it is helpful to see how many areas are impacted by the change.

Costs

Identification of each of the costs associated with the change. Consider dividing these into the costs directly associated with creating new ways of working, ie people, equipment, services, and the costs of managing the change. For example, the costs of establishing a team to coordinate the change and to support those involved. This might include your role, a 'Change Management Office' (CMO) of specialist planners, risk analysts, procurement experts and a training team to deliver training in the new ways of working.

These costs might include a charge for the office space used by the CMO and venue costs for the training. There may be some costs for managing the risks (see below), including the costs of creating and implementing the change in a sub-optimal way, ie not the cheapest way but the way that minimizes the risks.

Consider whether you want to include the opportunity costs of not carrying out other work whilst the change is taking place.

Risks

A risk is an uncertain event that if it should occur will have an effect on the achievement of the objectives of the change. Describe:

- the situation that would lead to an effect on the achievement of the change;
- what might cause this situation and how likely it is;
- what the indicators are that this situation is starting to occur;
- what the immediate effects of this situation would be on the achievement of the change and how severe these effects are deemed to be;
- what actions can be taken to minimize the chances that this situation will occur.

The acceptance criteria for an effective business case are:

- the benefits are described in sufficient detail that they can be used to decide which aspects of the change are essential and which would be advantageous but not responsible for the generation of specific benefits;
- the information about the costs is comprehensive and whilst estimates lack detail at the start of the change, there is a high degree of confidence that every expected area of cost has been included;
- proof that those defining the change have looked ahead at what might impede its progress and considered how these problems can be overcome.

Benefits description

The purpose of the benefits description is to ensure all those associated with the realization of the benefit understand what it is and how it is to be measured. The benefits description includes the information described in Chapter 4 on Business need, including:

- Detailed description of the type of benefit or disbenefit, and who is taking responsibility for its realization.

- Expected level of benefit, immediately after implementation, and once the change has been fully embedded. This is because it is unlikely that new ways of working will generate benefits immediately. Performance levels may fall initially as people struggle to remember how to do things differently, so it might be worth including an estimate of any decreases in levels of service ahead of the realization of the benefit.

- Relationship to other benefits, specifically:
  - benefits that this benefit relies upon and their origin, eg other parts of this change initiative or other projects or change initiatives taking place elsewhere in your organization or market place that create circumstances which enable this benefit to be realized;
  - benefits that this benefit contributes towards, strengthening the overall value of this benefit as without it you may lose the chance to create further benefits.

- How the benefit will be measured, ie actual or percentage amounts, and the data items to be measured, eg number of people, time elapsed, number of steps in a process, number of complaints or compliments, scores from surveys etc.

- Baseline measures from the existing business environment that will be used as a comparison of the measures taken after the change has been implemented. Find as many measures as possible that might be relevant to the benefit you are trying to prove, to give yourself the greatest chance of showing an improvement.

The acceptance criterion for a benefits description is: there is sufficient detail in the explanation of how the existing state has been measured that those planning the activities in realizing the benefits for Iteration 2 and onwards understand what they need to do.

Change management strategy

The purpose of the change management strategy is to explain how all of the change activities will be coordinated and managed. As the change evolves different people will become involved at different times so the change management strategy acts as a rapid induction. It provides guidance on:

Organization structure – the change management strategy should state that individuals are expected to take responsibility for their own change activities, as self-directed effort and willing collaboration with others is needed to successfully implement change. This section includes a description of the different roles that those impacted by the change will be expected to perform (see Appendix 1: Change roles) and how authority for decision making has been delegated through this structure to ensure that everyone feels sufficiently empowered to make changes to their way of working.

How risks and issues are escalated – whilst authority for making change has been delegated to those whose ways of working need to change, this must be balanced with an escalation process for when more authority is needed. It is important to agree from the start what constitutes an escalation item. An easy choice would be those risks that have been assessed as high probability and high impact, but this means that everyone has to have a similar understanding of what high impact means. Consider defining high impact as:

- additional work not previously considered part of the change requiring additional funding above X amount;
- any change activity that affects other parts of the business not previously included in the scope;
- any change activity that affects external parties (customers, suppliers, regulators) in a way that they have not already been warned about.

Balance with business as usual – guidance needs to be given on how individuals split their time between making changes and continuing with their business as usual responsibilities. In some cases staff may be formally seconded to the change initiative for its complete duration or for a specific iteration. Line managers of resources involved must agree to the backfilling arrangements or lower levels of performance for their team during the secondment period.

In the vast majority of cases staff will be asked to split their time between the two responsibilities and will need guidance on how to prioritize their work.

How quality of the work is checked – before implementing changes into the 'live' environment we need to know that their fitness for purpose has been assessed and that the change creates the specified outputs and does not disrupt other elements of the business environment.

Define if internal or external resources will be used in these quality reviews and describe the different tests that they will be asked to perform. Understanding this approach will help those creating the change management plan to identify the appropriate resources.

How progress is to be tracked and reported – describe what aspects of the change will be monitored to ensure that it will deliver what is expected. Using the roadmap described in this book, progress on activities will be tracked against time and achievements will be tracked by measuring the benefits and identifying what proportion of the old ways of working has been dismantled.

This section should explain who will receive regular progress information, how this will be made available to them and how their feedback will be incorporated into the change. This approach should also define any confidentiality or data security issues, specify, where appropriate, who can see what information, and clearly identify any information about the change that is not to be made publicly available.

The acceptance criteria for the change management strategy are:

- that line managers who may be asked to release staff for change activities have been consulted on the procedures for maintaining acceptable levels of business as usual during times of change;
- that the boundary between normal difficulties and situations that need to be escalated to more senior management is very clear;
- there is an explanation of where the change is managed in accordance with the organization's existing policies and procedures and where these are not being applied.

Change management plan

The purpose of the change management plan is to outline how the change will be delivered. Using the agile approach we will avoid creating a detailed plan of all the activities needed to implement the change because how the change takes place will evolve as small changes are made available to the users and they identify further actions. However, in order to manage the expectations of those involved and ensure that the necessary resources are available when needed, a plan must be created that includes the following information:

- Timeframe:
  - statement of the overall timeframe allocated to this change, and evidence that this has been decided in conjunction with the business and that it acknowledges any 'no-go' times;
  - how many iterations there are expected to be and what each of their expected outcomes are;
  - how the overall timeframe for the change will be divided across these iterations.

- Use of the processes defined in the roadmap – clarification on whether iterations will follow on consecutively from each other at the end of the process for realizing the benefits or soon after this process has commenced.

- Governance – allocation of specific activities needed to govern the change across each of the iterations. These activities will include regular progress reporting and reviews of risks and issues.

- Resources – what resources are required to identify, create, implement and quality review new ways of working and who will be responsible for collecting data about the new business environment to prove that benefits have been realized.

- Workstreams – clarification of the areas of the business involved in the change (based on the scope and exclusions within the description of the change) and an explanation of how work in these areas is to be managed, eg grouped together into workstreams.

- Assumptions – at this early stage it will be necessary to make some assumptions about how the change will evolve, and this will affect the number and duration of the iterations. These assumptions should be recorded and then these assumptions can be reviewed and updated at the end of each iteration.

- Constraints – there may also be some constraints that affect the iterations. For example, if there are times when the organization is particularly busy and changes are not allowed to take place, eg end of the financial year or during the heaviest trading periods, then these should be recorded as well so that these are taken into account now and at the end of iteration reviews.

The acceptance criteria for the change management plan are:

- that each of the iterations is short enough to create a focused period of work whilst being long enough to create meaningful changes;

- that taken together, all of the iterations will cover the scope and deliverables described in the change description.

Appendix 3
Communication activities

Change only occurs if those who have to work differently can be persuaded of the need for change and are given the opportunities to participate in the creation of the new ways of working. This results in a sense of ownership which motivates them to adopt the changes. Change leaders need to conduct a wide variety of communication activities throughout the whole lifecycle of the change to create initial support and participation and maintain it all the way through to the end of the change initiative.

Wherever possible, face-to-face communication is best (see Chapter 5: Relationship building, for some of the reasons why this is the case). In this appendix we will look at two types of change communication: 1) presenting information about the change – although in meetings and presentations we will try to build in opportunities for two-way communication, it is important to recognize that any presentation is essentially about telling and selling, and not necessarily engaging with the audience at a deep enough level to persuade them to think or act differently; and 2) workshops – facilitated discussions and activities that help people engage with the information about the change, internalize it and begin to apply it to their own circumstances, making it real for them.

Presenting information

In any presentation you need to consider what you want the outcome to be and ensure that all of the information that you make available supports this objective. A critical success factor in presenting information is recognizing that only a portion of your audience will hear what you are saying at that point in time. Although everyone is present, some of them will filter out your messages because they are not ready to hear them. Reasons for this could be that they think that the change does not affect them so there is no need to listen to any information about it, or they believe they already know what is going to happen so there is no need to listen.

To maximize the number of people who are paying attention, it is important to set your message in their context, so make sure that the information you are providing is relevant to your audience and has been tailored to reflect their responsibilities, their ways of working and the types of products, services, customers and suppliers that they are associated with.

It is important to recognize that even though you are making an announcement about the change, if there is no flexibility to incorporate feedback from your audience then you are in danger of your information sounding like an instruction that must be followed. Whilst a lot of the big decisions about your change may have to be taken without consultation, try to identify aspects for which you can ask your audience for their views, so that they feel included.

Case example

Rebecca announced to her team that their organization was merging with another organization. Whilst all of the big decisions about how the organizations would join up had already been taken at board level, she presented the details she had been given in such a way that encouraged her team to come up with ideas for how they could explain the merger to their customers, and how they could start planning 'get to know you' sessions with their counterparts in the other company.

Finally, it is very important to recognize that a great deal of the communication will take place after the presentation. There will be discussion about the information, opinions will be shared and those who are opinion formers will be listened to – often with more care and attention than your original audience gave your announcement! For this reason, think about how you can guide this informal information sharing:

- How can you ensure that the natural opinion formers are well briefed about the change?

- How can you make more detailed information available for people to review after your presentation?

- How can you put yourself in the loop so you are included when people are asking questions?

For example, on a number of occasions I have had to announce changes that generate shock and fear. This often involves a business unit being closed, or an organization that is re-locating, meaning many people will either lose their jobs or have to move hundreds of miles and uproot themselves from their families in order to keep their jobs.

I do a lot of preparation for these kinds of announcements because I know the pattern that they follow – it is surprising and feels almost counterintuitive. Once I have made the announcement I am no longer 'in the loop' and it is not a two-way conversation. I have given people shocking news that they need to come to terms with, and in the vast majority of cases the way in which they will do this is to turn to their own support networks for reassurance.

Even if I was close to these people, I will no longer be the one that they turn to. This can feel very isolating. In our business communications there is normally a response, comments and questions and people provide feedback so you can sense how they are feeling.

However, in my experience, the more serious the change, the less chance there is of feedback. One impact of no longer being involved is that it is difficult to know what details to make available – people ask each other questions about the impact of the change and they don't turn to me for answers. I have to guess what they need and make the information available in a way that enables them to access it when they need it.

Workshops

Workshops are a tried and tested technique for building teams, solving problems and creating consensus. Whilst they are often more effective than interviews or 'at desk' conversations, they are not free so they must be used appropriately. The costs of workshops include the fees for independent facilitators, venue and catering costs as well as the costs of lost production when people are at the workshop and not carrying out their day-to-day responsibilities.

For this reason it is a good idea to estimate how many workshops are going to be needed throughout the life of the change and include these costs in the overall budget for the change. To create your estimate, consider:

- the total number of people impacted by the change;
- the number of departments or functions involved, including external groups, eg customers, suppliers or regulators;
- the number of different aspects of the change that could be usefully workshopped (see below for the core workshops commonly associated with change initiatives).

When planning any workshop, remember that it is not a presentation, so whilst you will need to share some information about the subject, the majority of the time will need to be devoted to participation by those attending. The more participants you have, the longer it will take them to feed back their views to the others, so if you want to keep things short, you may have to restrict the number of participants.

A workshop is all about engagement in the subject by the participants, so it is important that whilst you prepare activities for them to become engaged in, you do not create a rigid timetable. It is more effective to spend time on the areas that participants feel are important rather than making sure that every activity you have created is undertaken.

Core set of change workshops:

Figure A3.1

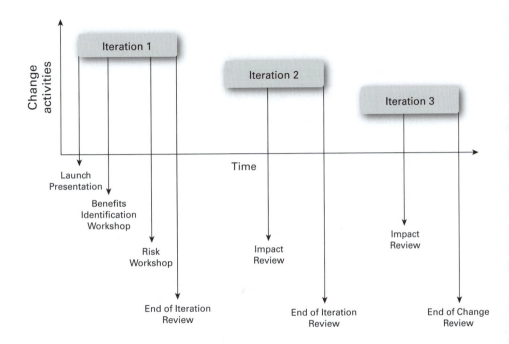

Launch presentation

Attendees:

- operational managers whose areas are subject to change;
- those involved in making changes to their ways of working;
- those who will be impacted by the changes but who are not expected to significantly alter how they work (might experience changes in who they work with or format or timing of when inputs become available for their use).

Structure of the event:

This event will have the most impact if it can be delivered face to face, with an opportunity for those involved in the change to ask questions and share their views. The objective of the presentation is to introduce the change as soon as possible so that those affected can come to terms with it, and address any concerns about the change and generate support for it.

Agenda:

- Explain how the change is connected with a wider change agenda across the organization.
- Outline the high level objectives and expected benefits of the changes.
- Give a broad overview of the scope of the changes, who is most likely to be impacted and areas where the change is not expected to be felt.
- If known, confirm the timeline for the changes and explain any changes this will have on the normal timetable of events, eg if any audits, training events etc are expected to be postponed whilst the change takes place.
- If known, acknowledge who is likely to be negatively impacted and what support these individuals can expect to receive.
- Outline the approach to the management of the change:
  - describe how their participation in the change will be welcomed;
  - explain that there is a roadmap for managing the change and that this will be made available to anyone who would like to see it;

- acknowledge that people will be asked to balance their involvement in the change alongside their existing responsibilities;

- reassure the audience of the depth and frequency of the communication they will receive.

Benefit identification workshop

Attendees:

- operational managers whose areas are subject to change;

- marketing, PR and/or advertising – a representative who can help identify benefits concerned with increased brand awareness and name recognition, positive market perception, and a higher and/or more positive media profile;

- finance – a representative who can calculate the financial benefits including revenue increases, tax breaks, fixed and operational cost reductions;

- sales and/or business development – a representative who can identify potential new opportunities as a result of the expected changes;

- HR – a representative who is responsible for performance measurement and can help to identify those measures already being recorded in the organization which can be used to prove that each benefit has been achieved;

- strategy office – a representative from the senior management team responsible for the analysis and planning of your organization's strategy and vision who is able to explain how the proposed changes will contribute to the achievement of the strategic objectives.

Structure of the event:

The purpose of this event is to encourage as wide a range of stakeholders as possible to define the positive impact of the change, either for the organization as a whole or for their specific area of responsibility. The facilitator should ensure that all benefit ideas are captured because benefits felt by one individual or that make a small financial or strategic contribution can still be a powerful influence when generating support for the change. As this is a workshop, the emphasis is on user participation so the agenda will encourage attendees to work together in pairs and small groups to identify and describe the benefits.

Example activity:

Divide the attendees into small groups and assign each group a specific element of the change, eg:

- streamlining a process;
- changing contract terms with a supplier to reduce costs;
- integrating several sources of data to reduce data entry costs.

Each group to answer the following questions about their change:

- What can we do that we could not do before? Is this a positive or negative effect?
- What will we no longer be able to do? Is this a positive or negative effect?
- What other changes does this change trigger? Is this a positive or negative effect?

Risk workshop

Attendees:

- operational managers whose areas are subject to change;
- marketing, PR and/or advertising – a representative who can help identify the potential negative effects of the change on brand awareness, market perception and media profile;
- sales and/or business development – a representative who can identify potential threats to existing customer relationships or the ability of the organization to win new business as a result of the expected changes;
- HR – a representative who can identify potential problems in relation to employment law or staff satisfaction or engagement as a result of the changes;
- strategy office – a representative from the senior management team responsible for the analysis and planning of your organization's

strategy and vision who is able to identify changes in the market or competitive landscape that could threaten the successful implementation of the change.

Structure of the event:

The purpose of this event is to identify what factors could prevent the successful implementation of the changes planned in each of the subsequent iterations, and how the proposed changes could threaten or enhance the capability or reputation of the organization in fulfilling its 'business as usual' responsibilities.

As this is a workshop, the emphasis is on user participation so the agenda will encourage attendees to work together in pairs and small groups to identify and describe the risks. This workshop can be combined with the benefits identification workshop.

Example activity:

Similarly to the benefits identification workshop, divide the attendees into small groups and present each of them with a proposed change. Ask them to answer the following questions:

- What could stop this change from being implemented successfully (eg insufficient resources, lack of training)?
- What negative effects could this change have on the capability or reputation of the organization?
- What actions should be taken to reduce the probability of problems occurring?
- What actions should be taken to reduce the impact if problems do occur?

End of iteration review/end of change review

Attendees:

- the person sponsoring the changes in this iteration;
- operational managers whose areas are subject to change;
- those who have created and implemented the changes.

Structure of the event:

> This is a meeting to find out whether the changes have worked, what other changes are now required as a result of them and what lessons can be learnt to improve the implementation of the next iteration. It is also an opportunity to confirm if the change initiative should continue, and if so who is best placed to be involved in the next iteration.
>
> If this review takes place at the end of the last iteration, it should concentrate on identifying the things that went well and should be repeated for future change initiatives, and those that went badly and ways in which they could be improved in future.

Suggested agenda:

- confirm that all items marked as completed on the prioritized requirements list have been successfully implemented;
- review the improvements reported by the users and update the benefits list;
- review the risk register and close off any that are no longer applicable;
- confirm that subsequent iterations are still required;
- confirm that the sponsor is the most appropriate person to sponsor the next iteration or agree a replacement;
- thank those responsible for designing and implementing the changes and confirm who is to be involved in the next iteration;
- review the productivity of this iteration and if necessary amend the change plan with new assumptions, constraints or scope of further iterations.

Impact review

Attendees:

- operational managers whose areas are subject to change;
- those involved in making changes to their ways of working.

Structure of the event:

The purpose of this meeting is to assess whether the effects of the changes are acceptable to the business area impacted by them. If the changes have caused disruption to existing processes or forced productivity below acceptable levels then further changes may be postponed whilst the business area takes remedial action or acquires additional resources to improve productivity, allowing more change to take place.

Suggested agenda:

Change can affect any area of the business so review these headings and add areas relevant to your organization:

- **Organizational efficiency** – impacting the flow of work through the department and the relationships with other departments.
- **Customer service** – impacting customer communication, speed and accuracy of fulfilling customer orders and enquiries.
- **Supplier relationships** – improving communication with the suppliers, providing up-to-date information on requirements.
- **Perception and reputation** – internally and externally. For example, does the department appear more organized and in control of its work?
- **Staff engagement** – are people engaging with the change?

Appendix 4
Change activity index

The purpose of this index is not to provide you with a list of all the documents that you are supposed to create or all of the meetings you are expected to attend as a change leader. Instead it is to help you understand the types of interaction with others and the work that you need to undertake yourself to ensure everyone knows what they are doing and to maintain the momentum of the change. It also recognizes that a considerable portion of your time will need to be spent on maintaining acceptable performance levels for 'business as usual' whilst creating the new ways of working.

Your specific responsibilities will dictate how your time is divided but for illustrative purposes, this activity index assumes that two-fifths of the time is spent on creating the change, one-fifth is spent on managing all of the change activities and two-fifths of your time remains on your business as usual role.

Figure A4.1

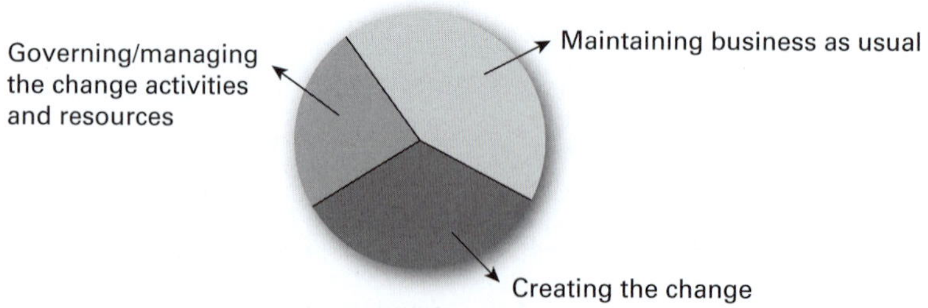

Governing/managing the change activities and resources

Maintaining business as usual

Creating the change

Maintaining business as usual

- define those activities that must remain stable during the period of change;

- identify those activities that will be temporarily stopped, undertaken by others or done to a lower level of performance;
- communicate these changes to internal and external customers;
- continue with day-to-day responsibilities;
- gather metrics on existing processes, business levels and performance measures that can be used as a comparison once the change has been implemented.

Creating the change

- Developing your understanding of the change. This involves:
  - acquiring expertise in the change through research and engagement with subject matter experts;
  - articulating the vision and direction of the change and setting it in the context of what it means for you.
- Devising new ways of working. You can do this by:
  - reviewing existing end-to-end processes;
  - re-imagining how work can be undertaken after the change.
- Participating in walkthroughs, workshops and pilots to devise the specifics of the change.
- Creating the inputs needed for new ways of working. You can do this by:
  - specifying the required deliverables;
  - participating in the projects that create these deliverables.
  - undergoing training to develop the skills needed in the new business environment;
  - practising new ways of working;
  - documenting new ways of working.
- Supporting others through the change. This involves:
  - articulating the vision and direction of the change in the context of what it means for those impacted by it;

- facilitating understanding of the change through workshops, meetings, discussions and presentations;
- creating a network of contacts and building relationships with those impacted by the change;
- bringing together those with common interests in the change to share experiences and knowledge;
- providing one-to-one coaching to those requiring specific support during the change;
- supporting participation in the change by delegating tasks and accountability for progress;
- managing conflict arising from the allocation of resources, direction of the change, attachment to the status quo etc.

Governing the change

- Create documentation to identify, scope and prove the viability of the change.
- Plan and re-plan the required change activities:
  - for creating the change;
  - for deploying the change;
  - for communicating the change.
- Establish the required funding for the change and create a cost schedule.
- Identify and acquire required resources for each activity.
- Monitor and control the progress of the change activities:
  - schedule;
  - budget.
- Report progress to those participating in the change and those impacted by it.
- Analyse, record and manage risks to the change initiative.
- Review and implement lessons learned from each completed activity or milestone.

Appendix 5
Change capabilities index

The purpose of the change capabilities index is to enable you to assess your own strengths and weaknesses in relation to leading change, and to consider how you can get the support that you need in areas where you have less experience.

This assessment of your capabilities should be reflected in your leadership framework described in Chapter 5. Before you begin your assessment, consider what activities you are responsible for (Appendix 4: Change activity index) and review your community map to remind yourself of those you need to lead through change.

To decipher whether you have a strong capability for change, you must be able to identify a number of situations where you have successfully demonstrated this skill or ability before. Within this exercise identify areas of change leadership where you don't feel you need any support, and are comfortable taking full responsibility for this area of change.

Where you possess some capability, recognize that whilst you may have been involved in this area of change leadership before, you are still learning and you are likely to benefit from the support and knowledge of others who are more experienced than yourself. You feel able to take responsibility for

Figure A5.1 How your change capabilities contribute to your leadership of change

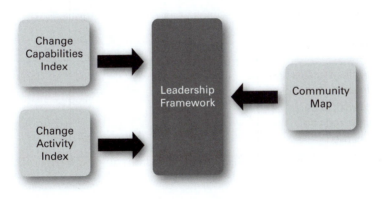

these areas of change, but you will need to check your progress and your impact and are willing to develop your approach as you learn more.

If the result of your assessment leads you to believe that you have no capability, this means you have no experience in this area of change and you may need coaching to develop your skills. You also recognize that if you are already at full capacity with other responsibilities it would be better to delegate this work to others with experience and ability.

Figure A5.2 Change capabilities index

	Level of capability		
	Strong capability	Some capability	No capability
Roadmap			
1. Can conceive of the change as a strategic initiative and identify its benefits for the organization			
2. Has a clear understanding of the drivers for change that exist outside of the organization			
3. Can conceive of the change as a series of tactical activities that must be planned, resourced and delivered			
4. Creates systems and structures to enable the work to be organized and controlled			

Figure A5.2 continued

	Level of capability		
	Strong capability	Some capability	No capability
5. Assesses the likely impact of each new way of working and understands when those affected are ready for change and when change needs to be delayed			
6. Assesses each of the change activities to understand their interdependencies with each other and their contribution to the achievement of the expected benefits			
7. Can explain the roadmap to others and get their support for its use			
Relationships			
8. Predicts where the impact of the change will be felt and identifies those affected			
9. Builds relationships with those affected			
10. Inspires trust and confidence in all those impacted by the change			

Figure A5.2 continued

	Level of capability		
	Strong capability	Some capability	No capability
11. Provides support for those fearful about their ability to adapt to the new ways of working			
12. Acts as a role model, adapting to the change early in the change lifecycle			
13. Is well respected by those affected by the change and has sufficient personal credibility to be seen as the leader of the change			
Environment			
14. Assesses readiness for change and addresses any shortfalls in capability ahead of implementation			
15. Identifies risks to successful implementation and creates appropriate mitigation actions and contingency plans			
16. Balances the energy needed to implement the change so that the participation in the change can be sustained until completion			

Resources

Achor, S (2010) *The Happiness Advantage*, Virgin Books, London

Ackerman Anderson, L and Anderson, D (2001) *The Change Leader's Roadmap*, Pfeiffer, San Francisco

Alexander Haslam, S, Reicher, SD and Platow, MJ (2011) *The New Psychology of Leadership*, Psychology Press, Hove

Allen, J (2011) *Team Leader: A guide to better management*, G2 Entertainment, Chelmsford

Anderson, C and Ackerman Anderson, L (2010) *Beyond Change Management*, Pfeiffer, San Francisco

Appelo, J (2012) *How to Change the World: Change management 3.0*, Jurgen Appelo, Rotterdam

Ariely, D (2009) *Predictably Irrational: The hidden forces that shape our decisions*, Harper Collins, London

Balogu, J and Hope Hailey, V (2008) *Exploring Strategic Change*, 3rd edn, FT Prentice Hall, Harlow

Champy, J (2010) *The 7 Rules of Change Management*, New Word City

Collins, P (2012) *The Art of Speeches and Presentations*, John Wiley & Sons, Chichester

Covey, SR (2008) *The Speed of Trust*, Simon & Schuster, New York

Davidson, A (ed) (2009) *1000 CEOs*, Dorling Kindersley Limited, London

Drucker, PF (2009) *Management Challenges for the 21st Century*, Harper Collins, New York

Duhigg, C (2012) *The Power of Habit*, William Heinemann, London

Edmondson, AC (2012) *Teaming*, Jossey Bass, San Francisco

Gerschel, A and Polsky, L (2013) *The 19 Steps to Lead Employees over the River of Change*, PeopleNRG, Princeton, NJ

Gerzema, J and D'Antonio, M (2013) *The Athina Doctrine*, Jossey Bass, San Francisco

Goleman, D (2006) *Social Intelligence*, Hutchinson, London

Goleman, D (2011) *Leadership: The Power of Emotional Intelligence*, More Than Sound, Northampton, MA

Goleman, D (2011) *The Brain and Emotional Intelligence: New insights*, More Than Sound, Northampton, MA

Grant, A (2013) *Give and Take*, Weidenfeld & Nicolson, London

Harvard Business School (2003) *Managing Change and Transition*, Harvard Business School Publishing Corporation, Boston, MA

Hefferon, K and Boniwell, I (2011) *Positive Psychology: Theory, research and applications*, Open University Press, Maidenhead

Kahneman, D (2011) *Thinking Fast and Slow*, Penguin, London

Kantor, RM (2004) *Confidence*, Random House Business Books, New York

Kates, A and Galbraith, JR (2009) *Designing Your Organization: Using the STAR model to solve 5 critical design challenges*, Jossey Bass, San Francisco

Lencioni, P (2002) *The Five Dysfunctions of a Team*, Jossey Bass, San Francisco

Lewis, S (2011) *Positive Psychology at Work*, Wiley Blackwell, Chichester

Lewis, S, Passmore, J and Cantore, S (2011) *Appreciative Enquiry for Change Management*, Kogan Page, London

Marr, B (2012) *Key Performance Indicators: 75 measures every manager needs to know*, Pearson: FT Publishing, Harlow

McCann, J and Selsky, JW (2012) *Mastering Turbulence*, John Wiley & Sons, San Francisco

Novak, D (2012) *Taking People with You*, Penguin, London

Orti, P (2012) *Thriving Through Change at Work*, Unusual Connections, London

Polsky, L (2013) *Say Yes to Change: 27 secrets to motivating yourself and your team during challenging times*, PeopleNRG, Princeton, NJ

Pullicino, M (2003) *Process Think: Leading to change and innovation*, MPI Publishing, Edderton

Ricci, R and Wiese, C (2011) *The Collaboration Imperative*, Cisco Systems, San Jose, CA

Richard Hackman, J (2011) *Collaborative Intelligence: Using teams to solve hard problems*, Berrett-Koehler Publishers Inc, San Francisco

Shaw, C, Debeehi, Q and Walden, S (2010) *Customer Experience: Future trends and insights*, Palgrave MacMillan, Basingstoke

Smith, P (2012) *Lead with a Story*, Amacom Books, New York

Smith, S and Milligan, A (2011) *Bold: How to be brave in business and win*, Kogan Page, London

Stavros, JM and Hinrichs, G (2009) *The Thin Book of SOAR: Building strengths-based strategy*, Thin Book Publishing, Bend, OR

Walter, TJ (2013) *It's my Company too*, Greenleaf Book Group Press, Austin, TX

Watkins, M (2003) *The First 90 Days*, Harvard Business School Publishing, Boston, MA

Williams, B (2012) *50 Top Tips for Managing Change*, Spearmint Books, Laxey, Isle of Man

Wiseman, L with McKeown, G (2010) *Multipliers: How the best leaders make everyone smarter*, Harper Collins, London

Ziegler, B (2011) *Collaborative Maxims: Principles for working together*, Ben Ziegler, Victoria, BC, Canada

Index

NB: page numbers in *italics* indicate figures or tables

Also available from **Kogan Page**